Muskie Mania

Muskie Mania

Ron Schara

Contemporary Books, Inc.
Chicago

Published by Contemporary Books, Inc.
180 North Michigan Avenue, Chicago, Illinois 60601
Manufactured in the United States of America
Library of Congress Catalog Card Number: 77-89059
International Standard Book Number: 0-8092-7997-5

Published simultaneously in Canada by
Beaverbooks
953 Dillingham Road
Pickering, Ontario L1W 1Z7
Canada

To Denise, who married a fisherman and wisely sought to understand rather than change him;

To Mom, who showed how to love fishing;

To Dad, who showed patience; and

To Minnesota's Muskies, Inc., which collectively represents the best of muskie fishing and—in the final analysis—the quality of a fisherman's time on earth.

Contents

Acknowledgments

No man writes a book alone. And neither did I. But how do you say "thank you" to so many who also have explored the world of the muskie? Some I have met; others I only know by name. But they are all special people: Gil Hamm, founder of Muskies, Inc.; Leon Johnson, the dedicated Wisconsin biologist who shared his muskie research with those who cared the most, the fishermen; Larry Porter, a Muskies, Inc., member and a biologist who compiled much of the research findings used in this book; Al and Ron Lindner, of the In Fisherman Society, who taught me to "think and fish" and who shared their muskie knowledge; Larry Ramsell, world records secretary for the Freshwater Fishing Hall of Fame; Art Moraski, the night fisherman; Homer LeBlanc, the troller; Bill Vint, friend and colleague, who sent his muskie notes after the second request; the 1976 Board of Directors of Muskies, Inc., who granted access and use of their muskie library and newsletters; Kathy Martin, the redhead, who had never heard about muskies until she typed the manuscript and now wants to go fishing; and, finally, my many muskie fishing partners who proved to me that if I was crazy so were they.

Introduction

I am greatly excited and largely confused: symptoms of a first-time book author.

Lordy, after writing newspaper outdoor columns for the better part of a decade, I sit here now confronted with the problem of how do you start writing a book.

On muskies, no less!

The most mysterious big game fish in the waters of North America, a fish that thousands before me and thousands after will chase with an unquenchable thirst. But only a chosen few will catch.

And who am I but only another muskie addict—like the other multitudes who storm the muskie haunts, flail stout rods and heave giant plugs and call it fun? The real description is work.

And who should write a book on the finned beast, the muskie? Am I qualified? Who is really qualified?

Someday I thought I'd write a book. Probably not about muskies. Probably memoirs of an outdoor writer's fortunes and failings afield. The bits and pieces that gather in a man's mind after a lifetime of hanging around the lake shores and beating paths in the bush. But, I thought, that book can wait until my typewriter at the Minneapolis *Tribune* had rusted into retirement.

Well, someday is here. My memoirs still are incomplete; my typewriter is well oiled; yet I'm pondering the first words in a book.

Two incidents—totally unrelated—brought about this undertaking.

The first happened about eight years ago. I met my first muskie. Well, not really. I met my first muskie fisherman and joined him for a day in the boat on Minnesota's Leech Lake.

The fisherman's name was Dick Knapp. A well-known angler, he came to my attention with overwhelming credentials and a devotion to stalking Leech Lake's muskies. He also was a nice guy.

Our meeting and the hunt for muskies that followed are indelibly etched in my mind. Everything happened just the way everybody said it would. It was the perfect first muskie fishing trip. We got nothing.

Dick was not surprised. It had happened before: nothing. He would spend many, many more agonizing days under a searing sun, with aching arms and dogged stick-to-itiveness, for the same reward. Nothing.

Observing his untiring dedication made an impression. No sane man suffers because it feels good. My friend Dick Knapp was willing to make the sacrifices because he knew something that, at the time, I didn't know.

Such behavior is rare among outdoorsmen. Oh, duck hunters frolic over marsh muck; turkey hunters cherish the morning darkness, and you'll see some grown men kneel and weep over an 11-inch brook trout fooled by a wet fly.

But the muskie, by its very nature, demands an eternal sacrifice; it fosters its own religion. You gotta believe or you don't get the reward.

Dick Knapp had the religion. He served his time and he got paid. A muskie over 40 pounds hangs in a glass case in his home.

That a man and a fish should have such an affair, that the infatuation should hold such a bond, told me something about not only the fish but the people called muskie fishermen. And the colorful duo also said something about life itself. Perhaps in a zany way. But, I believe, more seriously. If a man lives to fish muskie, or play golf, or work, or sip beer on Saturday afternoons, then he dies inside if it is no longer possible.

My own curiosity over what made the muskie men (and women) tick led to my own discoveries about the fish, about the fishermen. About myself.

Then a year ago David Burns, a Chicago talent scout for publishers and the like, called and asked if I'd be interested in writing a book.

I said I was. Sometime.

He asked, "What subject?" Then he added, "If it's the right subject we might like to have you do a book right away."

My reply came unexpectedly fast.

"On muskies," I blurted.

"Why muskies?" David asked.

"Well," I said, "the muskie is an interesting fish, the muskie fisherman is a character, and between the two I think it would be a fun book to write. . . ."

I thought about Dick Knapp, my first muskie fishing partner. And I thought of the muskies I'd seen since and the character fishermen I'd come to know, admire and, mostly, appreciate.

If a fish can make a man be both humble and a hero, if it can magnetize the soul and harness a fisherman's will, then the muskie also can make a man write a book.

I surrender.

Ron Schara
August 1976

Muskie Mania

Part I

Myths

1

The Mystique

In all of fresh water, there is no other fish like it.

Muskie!

Even the sound of its name has an urgency, a sense of excitement. To experienced muskie hunters, the name symbolizes boldness, strength, jaws of needle-like teeth, obstinance, giantism. And—to many of the same veterans—the name also means ultimate frustration.

To others the muskie is a secretive fantasy, a torpedo-shaped cross between a slinky alligator and a cunning woman, a fish that lurks in watery depths, seldom to be seen.

Nelson Bryant of the New York *Times* once wrote, "Fishing for muskellunge is like writing love letters that are never mailed. Your chances of success are limited but there is pleasure in the ritual."

Yet others see the muskie as a bold master of all fresh water, patrolling its domain with but one objective: to combine all smaller fish into one. Itself. And it does. Almost from day one. Hatchery-raised muskies consume thousands of other lesser fishes within days. Muskies—55,000 of them—only two to three inches long have been known to eat as many as 700,000 carp fry in three days.

Its prey must be alive. The muskie seldom, if ever, will touch dead food. In fact, muskies will starve rather than scrub the bottom leftovers. With a nickname like "Tiger of the Lakes," would you expect any less?

What's more, fishermen expect nothing from the muskie. They contract such things as "muskieitus," a disease of addiction. They'll spend 10 hours a day for a week and call it a success if but one muskie lands in the boat. Others are happy seeing a "follow"—a muskie behind the lure. And still others question whether muskies really exist. A Pennsylvania study once concluded that the average angler—even in good muskie water—spent 75 to 100 hours of fishing to waylay a keeper.

But even those who subdue the real thing cannot contain their nervous excitement. Their eyes do not want to believe. And when it happens it's seldom accidental. You have to chase muskies to catch one. Occasionally panfishermen—particularly in the spring—will tie into a muskie quite unintentionally. But such blind luck is definitely not a shortcut to putting a lunker on the wall.

The best muskie fishermen in the country need an average of about 10 hours per fish. And it gets longer if you're not the best. A Minnesota school teacher once admitted fishing for muskies for 27 years and catching but 13. But he was happy. For he clearly preferred to take one muskie over 100 other fish species.

Of such things are mystiques made.

But what *is* this fish, the one officially known as *Esox masquinongy*? Why is it an obsession—to select fishermen? What hold does it have? Noted naturalist-writer Jack Denton Scott calls the muskie the "greatest prize nature can bestow upon a fisherman."

Bob Hill, a Minnesota angler, once recalled an incident in which a small muskie got hooked lightly right at a boatside.

The surprised fish leaped, twisted and crash-landed into the boat, knocking itself out. Hill weighed the nine-pound muskie and released it after the fish regained its senses.

"Did I catch any muskies? No. But then, they didn't get me either," he said later of the incident.

Why does a fish receive such accolades?

The muskie is just a fish, you know. Though an impressive one. A long, sloping snout covering a massive set of dentures gives rise to a pair of wide-set, penetrating eyes. Its large head, representing nearly a fourth of the body length, is flat or even concave on top and of iridescent green. The back is broad and muscular. The remaining body, ranging in color from green-gold to brown-gray or even silvery, is steamlined.

Nature-designed for sudden bursts of speed of up to 30 miles per hour, the muskie is propelled by a long, powerful, V-shaped tail.

And to further fool the other fishes of the water, the muskie is usually camouflaged, almost melting into a weedbed. It's body sides contain dark spots or bars on a light background, like so many stems of aquatic pondweed.

The muskie even has a nasty grin, helped by a protruding jaw. The grin is real, however, as both jaws hold teeth, including the tongue.

Not even the northern pike, a close relative, is so finely tuned and equipped to dominate its watery world. And for sure, no fish demands as much of a fisherman's time. Not only in the water but in his thoughts and dreams as well.

There's an old rule of thumb: it takes 10,000 casts to catch a muskie. Novices chuckle at such an absurd estimate. But novices soon learn. This is one old rule that has more fact than fancy. It is all too accurate. Some grown, rational men and women have spent years of honest searching for a muskie. Not days. Years.

Of course the opposite happens. An occasional muskie fisherman will catch a lifetime of memories on the first attempt. But it does no good. The mystique lingers. There always is a bigger muskie to catch.

That challenge alone perhaps generates the mystique of the muskie. Only two other fish in fresh water—sturgeon and paddlefish—obtain a larger hulk than a muskie. But neither the sturgeon nor the paddlefish possesses its personality and spirit. The muskie wins hands down on all the attributes that turn normal anglers into bumbling idiots.

The fish is curious but cautious. You can see a dozen muskies in an hour and come home empty-handed. Pro fisherman Gary Roach, of the Lindy-Little Joe tackle makers, and I once raised 23 muskies in an afternoon on Wisconsin's Deer Lake. Yet we only hooked three. And two of those spit the treble hooks.

Muskies almost seem to enjoy following lures or plugs. Like it was a game. So much so that the measure of an angler's prowess is often counted in "follows."

But do not think it foolish. If you can't catch a muskie, the next best thing is seeing one. Few other fish have the nerve to trail an angler's lure to the boat, then stare at the source of the false meal. It almost appears as if the muskie had a hunch the fishy-looking plug was a fake. And as the clever fish sinks slowly out of sight, it appears to say, "I thought so."

Meanwhile, on the surface, the angler, momentarily shocked at the sight, goes into a dither and awkwardly thrashes his lure in crazy figure-eight patterns. He's hoping the muskie will reconsider. The muskie seldom does.

I do not know why muskies exhibit such a habit. And I hope no one ever does. To see a long, dark shadow with greenlike penetrating eyes trail inches behind your ready hooks is a breathtaking, heart-stopping, knee-shaking, one hell of an experience.

Perhaps, above all else, it is the muskie's elusiveness, the close follows, the near misses, the massive sizes that make muskie fishing for most addicts.

But whatever the ingredients, the muskie mystique is real. It exists in the minds of the muskies' adversaries, the fishermen. And it will continue to exist far beyond the day when each angler has made his own last cast, beyond the day when the smartest muskie falls to a hook.

For in the end, and through eternal memories, the muskie does it all:

It can snap 30-pound monofilament the way the wind parts a twig, or it can fall to the delicate strength of an ultra-light rod and reel.

It will leap like an ornery marlin or dive like a sluggish catfish.

It will strike at high noon in a blinding sun or clobber a muskrat by the light of the midnight moon.

It will pulverize a plug on the surface or inhale a jig at 80-foot depths.

It will thrive in lakeshore weedbeds or lurk in a river's boulders.

It will fight like an alley cat or surrender like a watered log.

But of such things is the mystique made. For every angler who has ever tossed a muskie plug will come away impressed. He may become an addict. He may become bored. He may become exhausted or uncontrollably ecstatic. He may wish he'd never heard of a muskie. Or he may regret not having met such a fish earlier in life.

Whatever, the fisherman will feel something about this magnificent pike, good or bad, sad or happy. And for that, generations of fishermen yet to come can be assured that the mystique of the muskie will live on.

And that, my angling fellows, is good.

2

Tales Tall and Short

And so I came to where the muskellunge lay
And felt its river wetness,
Saw its dark green back, deep with silence,
Its belly white as sleet, weaving with the river muscular and tough.
And for a time I saw that fish rage with its violent cargo of teeth. . . .

—"Muskellunge," by Harry Humes

Only two kinds of muskies exist in the minds of most muskie fishing addicts: big sonabitches and little sonabitches.

If that assessment seems rather crude, if not indecent, the muskie has only itself to fault. Since the day sport fishing discovered the muskie, the fish has successfully managed to confuse, confound and otherwise baffle its aggressors, the fishing man.

But do not misunderstand. When a muskie fisherman glances into the blue-green waters and his eyes fall upon the silent shadow of a muskie on the follow; when the excitement has ended and the anticipation has drained; when the muskie fisherman sighs and says, "That was a big sonabitch!"—friends, the words come from the heart. No finer testimonial to the muskie has ever been uttered.

And it doesn't take long before most fishermen can sing the praises of the muskie. A first-time muskie novice immediately senses the mystery of it all, wondering what he is supposed to look for in the first place and wondering if he'll recognize what it is if he sees it.

Of course old-time muskie hands know what's happening—they've seen muskies, they've located the haunts—still they also frequently wonder: "What am I doing here?"

7

Then they go back and continue the search.

And the novice? He, too, will return. Something will happen. Something will hatch a memory. A swirl. A snapped line. A smashed plug. Something will happen. Maybe a giant muskie (aren't they all?) will cruise alongside the boat, roll by the transom and eyeball the prop on the outboard.

It's happened. And will happen again. But the novice will not want to believe. Yet he must. For his eyes do not lie.

It is the unpredictability of the muskie that flavors the sport. Almost unbelievable unpredictability. Consider the surprise of an Illinois fisherman who, while visiting Wisconsin, hooked a 13-pound muskie on a chilly November day at 3 P.M. while the air temperature was but 28 degrees (F) and the wind sailed from the north. And it was snowing.

The story begs the questions: What was the muskie thinking? What was the fisherman thinking? Grown men normally avoid fishing below freezing temperatures unless there's ice on the lake, a shanty on the surface and a hot toddy on the stove.

But that's the muskie and the muskie fisherman. Unpredictable. A young Minnesota walleye fisherman, using 10-pound line and a one-eight-ounce jig, nabbed a small walleye a couple of summers ago, only to see a big muskie inhale the whole package. After the fight ended, a 31-pound, 50-inch muskie had fallen to an eighth-ounce piece of lead, leaving one walleye unquestionably terrified.

Or imagine the surprise of a Minnesota outboard motor mechanic who visited Leech Lake to fix a friend's ailing craft. They repaired the motor, had a few beers and tossed out a couple of fishing lines, adorned with small fathead minnows. Minnows three inches long at most.

The hooked bait was aimed at some unsuspecting walleye. Instead a 51-pound, one-ounce muskie chomped down on the tiny morsel and one of the largest muskies ever to come out of the lake was about to be caught.

However, a young water-skier on Lake St. Clair in Michigan may have experienced the most unusual of all surprises. The water-skier, a young man, took a spill on the famed muskie lake. No problem. Lots of skiers fall. But the legs thrashing in the water attracted a rather aggressive muskie. The fish attacked.

Both legs received deep tooth cuts and scratches before the fish got discouraged. The incident marks one of the few known human attacks by a muskie, although the fish often has been seen swimming among bathers on lake beaches.

Gil Hamm, the founder of Minnesota's Muskies, Inc., has of course heard of various hair-raising experiences with the elusive fish. He's also felt a few. T'was a few years back when Hamm in the excitement of a muskie chase plunked his rump down on a boat seat that was covered with a giant Suick plug and three massive treble hooks. There's no need to describe the exact location of Hamm's wound. But his partner, Bud Gustafson, was called upon to remove the lure and repair the damage. This was done in the boat after the appropriate clothing was removed. And once the task was finished the pair resumed fishing. Muskie fishermen have no price for glory.

But of all the tales and tribulations about muskie fishing, none matches the events that began on a hot, muggy July day on Minnesota's Leech Lake.

The year was 1955. Fishing generally had been poor throughout much of the early summer and, as usual, anglers were complaining. The big lake was calm that day, not a stitch of wind. Fishing guide Warren Bridge had a party of anglers out on his launch. A muskie rolled on the surface. Bridge spotted the movement and trolled a plug through the rippled water. The muskie struck.

In other bays on Leech Lake the same scene was being repeated. Suddenly muskies were hitting everywhere and everything. In two days 27 muskies were hauled into the scales. The largest went 42 pounds, six ounces.

The word spread like hot butter. Another fishing guide, Merle Wescott, and his party nailed nine huge muskies for a total of 204 pounds. They had fished for four hours and had 25 strikes.

During the week of July 25, more than 140 large muskies were taken out of Federal Dam alone—just one area of Leech Lake.

The fishing docks buzzed with excitement; boat rentals were at a premium; the entire lake was a madhouse as fishermen scurried about in search of their own dream, a trophy muskie.

For two weeks the bonanza continued. Muskies gone mad. And when it ended some 163 or so muskies, ranging in size from 19 to 43 pounds, had been caught.

Then, as suddenly as it started, the madness ended. They called it "The Muskie Rampage" or "Muskie Uprising." And as time passed they began to refer to the episode as "the year the muskies went nuts."

But to this day no one knows why. Some say it was the weather. But there have been hot, muggy days since. Some say there was a crowded supply of muskies in the lake at the time and that they had overeaten their natural food supply. Others, scientists and laymen alike, simply cannot venture a guess.

All possible explanations have been examined. Still there is no answer, no reason.

All anybody knows is that the Muskie Rampage of 1955 did happen. It was the year that the muskies went nuts.

And it's hard to believe.

But a lot of things about muskies are like that.

3

Catching the Fever

The fever does exist.

Not all anglers catch it; a few are even immune. But anybody who has ever pursued the muskellunge will begin to show symptoms. And if, by chance, the symptoms are unchecked and further dealings with the muskie come about, the fever will take over.

That's guaranteed. The muskie has a magnetism possessed by few other sports critters. And I know of no fishermen who, once touched by the fish's magic, have ever forgotten the experience. They may quit muskie fishing; they may catch that once-in-a-lifetime trophy; they may find more rewards in casting dry flies to wary brown trout. But they will not deny that the fever exists.

Knowing that there is such a muskie cult, a dedicated brotherhood, an unquenchable appetite connected with the sport is of little value in avoiding the fever. If you play with matches long enough you'll get burned. And if you try for muskies often enough you'll get hooked.

I know. For I fought the fever. I ignored the muskie and snickered at its addicts. And after my first outing for muskies, the day was so uneventful I even wondered if muskie fishermen everywhere were playing with full decks.

But then came muskie fishing trip number two.

A neighbor, Jack Lundgren, is an unassuming man, a building con-tractor who works and plays hard. And in his sweat-stained hat and sawdust-covered work clothes, there was little hint that there also walked a confirmed muskie addict. Not that he tried to hide his in-fatuation with the fish. Except I once thought muskie addicts had to have certain qualifications. What kind I did not know. But, I thought, the addicts somehow came from abnormal walks of life.

That is not true. Likewise, there are no qualifications for being crazy about muskies. Fish for them once or a hundred times and you can be obsessed. Make a million or live on food stamps. The muskie isn't particular.

Jack, the neighbor, eventually suggested a fishing trip, of course. For muskies, of course. And I accepted, of course. And if any mistake was made on my own road to catching the fever, that second trip was it.

Jack had a cabin on Minnesota's Little Boy Lake and he knew the water well. But it didn't matter. For the first half day or so, my second attempt at muskies was exactly like the first. Nothing happened.

But then it happened on a cast no different from the hundreds made before it. The plug was an Eddy Bait, a chunk of wood really, shaped like a fat-headed torpedo. And the water to which the plug was tossed was no more muskie-looking than the acres of other aquatic fields.

Like a well-oiled robot I jerked the plug, reeled in the slack line, jerked the plug, reeled in the slack line—when, quite simply, all hell broke loose 15 feet from the boat. The water around the plug erupted into a violent swirl; a wide-pointed, red-tinted tail flashed out of the ripples. My rod heaved from the collision. And, if I remember cor-rectly, my eyeballs bounced off the boat deck . . . or could have. In a reflex action, I hauled back on the rod. And for a moment it was a standoff. The muskie had the plug and was not about to let it go. And I had not yet been yanked over the gunwales.

But as quickly as turmoil began, it also ended. My line went limp. The muskie was gone. And so was the Eddy Bait, thanks to a faulty wire leader.

Nor was there time to analyze what happened. It was a good-sized muskie but I know not how good. That didn't matter. I had met my first muskellunge.

And I remember hearing Jack chuckle. He hadn't seen many wire leaders break, but nothing surprises a muskie fisherman. But he wasn't laughing at wire leaders. He was witnessing the first telltale antics of a fellow angler about to get the fever.

And it got worse after that. On the very next day, a dark green slender shadow trailed my bucktail spinner as it churned toward the boat. The shadow had eyes. Big eyes. And I swore those eyes were six-inches apart. Another encounter with the muskie. That meant I had contacted, or otherwise stumbled into, two muskies in three days of fishing.

Some people might conclude that such a rate of action ranks muskie fishing only slightly above watching paint dry.

But, friends, its different. Paint doesn't stare back at you. In the lulls between contacts with a muskie, there is a tremendous amount of energy spent. Cast and cast. And cast some more. Work this lure; work that lure. Yank and twitch and otherwise force your angling spirit to continue on. If you succeed and keep trying, you are coming down with the fever. If the dry spells no longer bother you, you have the fever. No doubt.

Anyway, the muskie took a look, then slowly settled out of sight. And I, excited by seeing such a phenomenon, reared back and continued to make more casts. Meanwhile Jack maintained his casting pace.

Later that afternoon—with a brisk westerly breeze—we drifted alongside a deep-water weedbed, adjacent to a dense shoreline stand of bulrushes. Jack was using a jerk bait, a Suick. If I remember right, the color was an off-white.

So far his efforts had been rather uneventful. I had had the one muskie strike and a follow. But he knew he'd have his day in court. Muskie addicts are like that. Prolonged periods of actionless fishing, to a muskie enthusiast, simply mean that "it won't be long now." (Addicts repeat that phrase again and again.)

This time Jack was right.

Again with no warning, a silvery flash tore up out of the submerged weed stems and gracefully nabbed Jack's defenseless Suick plug. He set the hooks and the fight was on. But it was not a big fight—not yet, anyway.

"It's a small one," Jack shouted. The muskie rolled near the boat, trying to escape the hooks, and gave us both a long look.

"He might go 30 inches," said Jack.

Suddenly the small muskie dived for the depths. Jack yanked back, trying to land the fish quickly to release it.

The small muskie wouldn't budge. Jack's heavy rod and monofilament clearly was sufficient to manhandle a 30-inch muskie. Still the fish wouldn't give an inch.

"It must be tangled in the weeds," I instructed. "That's all it could be."

Jack agreed and leaned harder into his rod. Suddenly the small muskie popped to the surface. Jack swung the fish into the boat like it was a bluegill.

That's when we both noticed a pair of long, fresh gashes on the muskie's back near the dorsal fin. The two cuts were still bleeding.

Jack looked up at me.

"Do you know what those are?" he asked, referring to the cuts.

My face was blank.

"Another muskie had a hold of this little guy," he said, matter-of-factly.

"Do you think so?" I wondered.

"That's all it could be," said Jack. "Yessirr . . . there's a big one down there someplace that's willing to eat a 30-inch muskie."

I let Jack's words soak in for a few seconds.

I was almost hesitant to make another cast. Not far from the weed-bed, a group of young boys played and frolicked on a camp beach. I wondered if they knew what giants roamed the waters.

For a few minutes I dreamed that I indeed had hooked such a fish. Wouldn't that be the thrill of a lifetime?

I picked up my rod. I was excited. The strike could come at any minute. That thrill of a lifetime, that magnificent fighting trophy could be mine on the very next cast.

And that, my friends, is what the fever is all about.

4

Quest for a World Record

The year was 1957.

It was about 11 A.M. on a cool, hazy Sunday morning—September 22—in the Thousand Islands section of the St. Lawrence River.

At that moment a six-inch wooden plug, trolled by Art Lawton in about 25 feet of water, passed within reach of the largest muskellunge ever officially landed on hook and line.

The massive fish had lived for 30 years. But on that famous day its gaping jaws opened and smashed into the lure. Lawton's 18-foot rowboat slowed to a halt. For an instant Lawton, a refrigeration specialist from Delmar, New York, thought he had snagged the bottom.

But then the snag began to throb. And Lawton, who had taken many muskies over 30 pounds, knew for sure he had a dandy.

The big fish rolled on the surface a few times but never jumped. Lawton let the fish take line whenever it wanted. He was in no hurry. The minutes ticked away.

Finally it was nearing noon; almost an hour had passed since the plug and the muskie collided. Gradually, Lawton tenderly nursed the huge muskie near the boat. The toothy beast began to wallow. A two-pound northern pike was coughed up. Lawton's wife, Ruth, reached for a gaff.

A new muskellunge world record was about to be set: 69 pounds, 15 ounces with a 64½-inch length and a 31¾-inch girth.

Lawton, of course, didn't know that.

He and his wife packed the fish in the trunk and headed back. He placed the muskie in a cooler where he worked and went home to bed.

On Monday morning he went to work. Finally that afternoon, 30 hours after the fish was caught, Lawton and friends went to Walter Dunn's slaughterhouse to weigh the muskie.

Everybody watched the scale. "Sixty-nine pounds, 15 ounces," said Dunn. The witnesses checked the scale and signed an affidavit.

No one mentioned world record. No one mentioned mounting the fish. Lawton didn't like mounted fish, nor did he have the money for the job. Thus, once it had been weighed, Lawton had no further thoughts about the fish except to give the meat to friends.

This he did, and so it is that the biggest muskie ever taken in sport fishing history was butchered.

Such an ending for the world-record muskellunge is perhaps only fitting. For many strange happenings have occurred in the quest for the world record.

A Michigan angler, Percy Haver, and a Wisconsin fisherman, Louie Spray, literally had a two-man battle for the world's title from about 1939 to 1949. Each man held the distinction twice until Spray took the lead with a 69-pound, 11-ounce record in 1949 out of Wisconsin's famed Chippewa Flowage. Spray's record stood for eight years until Lawton's famous catch came in four ounces heavier.

The World Record Listing*

Year	Weight	Fisherman	Lake/River	Date
1911	48 lbs.	Dr. Fredrich Whiting	St. Lawrence River	Unknown
1916	51 lbs.	F. J. Swint	Chief Lake (Wis.)	July 18
1919	51 lbs., 3 oz.	J. A. Knobla	Unknown	Sept. 13
1929	52 lbs., 12 oz.	E. A. Oberland	Lake Pogegama (Wis.)	July 1
1929	53 lbs., 12 oz.	Gordon Curtis	Lake of the Woods (Ont.)	Aug. 25
1931	56 lbs., 8 oz.	J. W. Collins	Lake of the Woods (Ont.)	July 24

1932	58 lbs., 4 oz.	George Neimuth	Lake of the Woods (Ont.)	Sept. 24
1939	58 lbs., 14 oz.	Percy Haver	Lake St. Clair (Mich.)	June 29
1939	59 lbs., 8 oz.	Louie Spray	Grindstone Lake (Wis.)	July 27
1939	60 lbs., 8 oz.	John Coleman	Eagle Lake (Ont.)	Oct. 3
1940	62 lbs., 8 oz.	Percy Haver	Lake St. Clair (Mich.)	June 28
1947	64 lbs., 8 oz.	Alois Hanser	Favil Lake (Wis.)	May 17
1949	67 lbs., 8 oz.	Cal Johnson	Lake Couderay (Wis.)	July 24
1949	69 lbs., 11 oz.	Louie Spray	Chippewa Flowage	Oct. 20
1957	69 lbs., 15 oz.	Art Lawton	St. Lawrence River	Sept. 22

*Compiled by Larry Ramsell, world records secretary, National Freshwater Fishing Hall of Fame.

The list of course does not tell of the close calls, the also-rans, the mighty catches that deserve recognition for their mere size. Undoubtedly the most impressive list of mammoth muskie catches is held by a pair of husband-and-wife fishing teams: World Record Holder Art Lawton and wife Ruth; and Len Hartman and wife Betty.

Between 1944 and 1968, the Lawtons and the Hartmans, both fishing the St. Lawrence River, boated more muskies of 40 pounds or more than anyone in history. Only those fish entered in the *Field and Stream* contests were counted.

In that time Lawton had three muskies over 60 pounds, including the world record. And his wife, Ruth, bagged two over 60 pounds, including a 68-pound, 5-ounce beauty—the third largest muskie on record!

The Hartmans, meanwhile, were not far behind. Len's biggest in 1961 was 67 pounds, 15 ounces, yet it placed second in that year's contest to Ruth Lawton's 68-pounder. Betty's best catch also came in 1961 with a 60-pound, 2-ounce trophy.

But since then, Len Hartman has captured nearly every line-weight record for muskies established by The International Spin Fishing Association, including the fly-rod category (31 pounds, 10 ounces). Hartman has taken a nine-pound, six-ounce muskie on a ¾-pound-test spinning line. And his best fish, 67 pounds, 15 ounces, fell to 11-pound test line.

All told, the Hartmans and the Lawtons have recorded 13 muskies over 40 pounds, 13 over 50 pounds and 10 muskies over 60 pounds. That's two more than all the other 60-pound-plus muskies reported.

There can be no doubt that the two couples have established a muskie catch record that is almost unbeatable. For there also is no doubt that 60-pounders are getting harder to find.

Wisconsin, which has the majority of former world records, has not produced a 60-pounder since Louie Spray found one in 1949. In 1975, a Wisconsin fisherman, Gene Allen, boated a 51-pounder out of Flambeau Lake, using a Bobbie Bait. That was the largest muskie reported in the state in 22 years.

Minnesota's state record of 54 pounds even was set back in 1957 on Lake Winnigoshish. One of the largest since then was a 51-pound, 1-ounce beauty out of Leech Lake, caught in 1973.

Ontario's famed Eagle Lake produced a province record in 1940 with a 61-pound, 9-ounce giant. But that Ontario record is still standing more than three decades later.

Does that mean there are no more 60-pound-plus giants stalking the continent's muskie haunts?

It is difficult to tell. If you listen to a muskie fisherman describe the size of muskies that followed or escaped a hook every year, a hundred new world records must still be at large.

Tales of giants are not new to the history of muskies, of course. Fish larger than Lawton's world record have been known in the minds of men for decades.

In 1788, a bunch of folks gathered for a Fourth of July celebration in Ohio and dined unceremoniously on a baked 100-pound muskie that had been netted in the Muskingum River. Or so the story goes.

A 102-pound muskie reportedly was trapped by Wisconsin fisheries workers in 1902. They found the giant in a spawning net set in Lake Minocqua. The fish was weighed and then released. Or so the story goes.

Michigan was not to be denied for giant tales, either. In 1914 or

1918, another net hauled in a 110-pounder out of Intermediate Lake. Or so the story goes.

The grandest muskie tale of all took place in Lake Michigan in the 1880s, when a commercial fisherman pulled in 162 pounds of muskellunge. Or so the story goes.

But events of long ago need not be discarded as pure imagination. Later in the 1950s t' skull of the so-called 162-pounder was discovered. The fish repo...edly was seven feet long. Its skull was 13 inches long and 20 inches in circumference.

Wisconsin remains the hotbed of muskie legends, however. The state has held the world record six times and most of the fishing citizenry remain convinced the record will "return home" one of these days.

They can't afford to claim otherwise. Muskie fishing is big business in the tourist-minded state. When Al Hanser set a new Wisconsin state record in 1947 with a 64-pound, 8-ounce muskie, a businessman, Ralph "Bottles" Capone, paid $1,800 to display the fish in his tavern for three weeks.

Capone's tourist attraction undoubtedly paid off. Every angler who has ever thought about muskies could sit and stare at Hanser's grand catch, order another beer or two, and simply dream that his day would come.

And plenty of them dream. A Wisconsin tourism study once indicated that nearly a fourth of its out-of-state visitors chose Wisconsin because of its muskies. And no doubt Wisconsin—with the largest muskie hatcheries in the world at Woodruff and Spooner—also can claim to harbor the highest muskie population in the world.

Someday, somewhere, maybe one of those fish will live long enough and grow fast enough to give Wisconsin the world's title again.

But while Lawton's world record has been held longer than any previous world muskie title, new state records are relatively common.

Since 1970, new records have been established in Ohio, Kentucky, Tennessee, Iowa, Virginia, Missouri, North Dakota, Illinois and New Jersey. The largest of these was Ohio's new 55-pound, 2-ounce record muskie.

Most of these states have one thing in common: They have recently introduced or re-established muskie populations. Hence as the years pass after the start of a successful muskie management program, the records start to fall.

The successful introduction of the hybrid muskie (a cross between a muskie and a northern pike) and the recognition of the hybrid as a separate record category also raise the possibility of a new world record.

The current hybrid world record of 50 pounds, 4 ounces, is held by Delores Ott Lapp. The fish was taken in Wisconsin's Lac Vieux Desert. North Dakota and Michigan also have recognized the hybrid and have state records of 40 pounds and 31 pounds, respectively.

Again, as the hybrid program continues, it is reasonable to expect that somewhere, someplace, some fisherman will set the hook on a new world record.

State Records*
Muskellunge (*Esox masquinongy*)

State	Weight	Fisherman	Lake/River	Date
N.Y.	69 lbs., 15 oz.[1]	Arthur Lawton	St. Lawrence River	9-22-57
Wis.	69 lbs., 11 oz.[2]	Louie Spray	Chippewa Flowage	10-20-49
Mich.	62 lbs., 8 oz.[2]	Percy Haver	Lake St. Clair	6-28-40
Ont.	61 lbs., 9 oz.	Ed Walden	Eagle Lake	10-8-40
Ohio	55 lbs., 2 oz.	Joe D. Lykins	Piedmont Lake	4-12-72
Penn.	54 lbs., 3 oz.	Lewis Walker, Jr.	Conneaut Lake	1924
Minn.	54 lbs. 0 oz.	Art Lyons	Lake Winnigoshish	1957
W. Va.	43 lbs.	Lester Hayes	Elk River	1955
Kty.	42 lbs.	Glen Terell	Licking River	2-23-73
Tenn.	42 lbs.	Dr. B. H. Holeman	Dale Hollow Reservoir	1-5-75
Iowa	38 lbs.	Ed Feldhacker	West Okoboji Lake	9-12-75
Va.	34 lbs., 10½ oz.	Richard Boone	Smith Mountain Lake	2-28-76
Mo.	27 lbs., 4 oz.	Hugh A. Palmer	Pomme De Terre	4-15-75
Vt.	23 lbs., 8 oz.	Richard Gross	Missisquoi River	1970
N.D.	22 lbs., 8 oz.	C. Kleve	Lake Williams	1975

Ill.	22 lbs.	Richard L. Emmons, Jr.	Spring Lake	5-6-73
Ala.	19 lbs., 8 oz.	Steve Leatherwood	Below Wilson Dam (Tenn. Riv.)	12-31-72
N.J.	19 lbs.	John Fleming	Delaware River	1970
Ind.	12 lbs.	Jim Vinyard	Little Blue River	1965
Md.	12 lbs.	Stephen R. Selman	Conowingo Dam	----

Muskellunge Hybrid
(*Esox masquinongy* x *Esox lucius*)

Wis.	50 lbs., 4 oz.[1]	Delores Ott Lapp	Lac Vieux Desert	6-28-51
N.D.	40 lbs.	Marvin Lee	Gravel Lake	1975
Mich.	40 lbs. 15 oz.	Kemp Gorenfle	Lake Michigamme	1976

Key:
1 = All Tackle World Record (current)
2 = Former World Record
* courtesy National Freshwater Fishing Hall of Fame

And how will it be caught?

Trolling, most likely.

Trolling has no particular magic over casting as a fishing technique. But the record shows that nearly all of the giant muskellunges have fallen to a lure that's been trolled, not cast.

And of course the most famous of the trollers are the Lawtons and the Hartmans.

Lawton seldom casts because he is convinced (and who wouldn't be, with his record?) that the largest muskies are found in deep water. And it is difficult to cast and effectively work deep water.

As a troller, Lawton uses a heavy five and one-half- to six-foot rod with a star drag reel and a 30-pound test line. A long braided steel leader is used ahead of the lure, along with a two-ounce lead sinker (bead chain style).

While he uses a variety of lures, Lawton's favorite is the six- to 12-inch solid Pikie of various colors, such as yellow, orange and red with green and blue in combinations. Lawton often paints his own lures.

When the world record opened its jaws, Lawton was trolling in about 25 feet of water with the plug riding about 18 to 20 feet down. To reach that depth, Lawton had about 125 feet of line played out behind his boat.

The world's champ also prefers to troll with, not against, the current.

Hartman, who holds many line records for muskies, established those records while trolling and casting. However, he, like Lawton, believes that trolling seems to produce the largest fish.

Hartman uses similar tackle, but he prefers to take a zig-zag trolling course to cover more water. He also trolls with the current and in deep water, 15 to 35 feet. As for lures, Hartman has no qualms about trying a couple of muskie lures together in tra.n fashion, such as a bucktail in front of a plug.

Of course every angler has pet methods and techniques. But the strange similarities between the techniques of Lawton and Hartman should give pause to every hopeful fisherman.

If there is a pattern for giant muskies—and Hartman and Lawton have more giants than anybody—it would appear that trolling deep is the basic clue. Lakes have no currents to speak of, hence their trolling pattern on the St. Lawrence River would not apply.

The two also use large plugs, but then most muskie fishermen usually do.

However, trolling deep is nothing particularly new. Anybody who trolls sooner or later will drop off into deeper water than intended.

In other words, on any given day there may be dozens of fishermen who knowingly or unknowingly are matching the very technique that produced Lawton's world record.

Of course not every troller fishes the former home of the world record, the St. Lawrence River. But then who knows if the river holds another record muskie, larger than 69 pounds, 15 ounces?

Who knows if any water holds a greater catch?

Nobody does really. But every muskie fisherman has that dream: That Lawton's record will someday fall. And indeed it might.

But in the meantime, let the airy hopes continue.

Muskie fishermen would have it no other way.

Part II

Muskies

5

Rebirth of Spring

Winter retreats grudgingly from most of muskie country. From November to March—almost half of the sun's year—the lakes and rivers are sealed in ice and covered with a blanket of snow.

And down below that frozen barrier, life among the cold-water inhabitants moves at a snail's pace in almost absolute silence, broken only by the groans and moans of shifting ice.

For predator and prey, it is not a time of great activity. The demands of the body metabolism have slowed greatly. And while food is necessary, the quantity and frequency of meals is reduced almost tenfold.

For Mama, a Leech Lake muskie, winter is a particularly drowsy season. She does not feel the urges of summer, when a meal a day is required to fulfill her energy needs. Sometimes that daily appetite would equal almost 10 percent of her body weight. But in winter, such gorging is unnecessary. One good-size perch or sucker will last for days or even weeks. Hence, most of her winter days are spent largely doing nothing but lying in the depths.

But the days gradually lengthen and the added warmth of the sun eats away at the frozen shield. The nights stay warmer, too, slowly but surely gnawing at the blue ice and weakening its crystalline strength.

The snow is first to go. And now the ice, having lost its insulating cover, must face an even warmer sun. Soon the ice itself blackens—hereby speeding its own demise by absorbing the sun's rays—and then, as if by magic, the rock-hard icecap is gone, as though it never had been. And once more the warming winds of spring ripple the waters that are no longer stiffened or entombed.

Increased life also returns to the shores of Leech Lake. In Portage Bay—where Mama has spent the winter—the shallow bays begin to warm first. And life congregates there.

Red-winged blackbirds—the males aggressive in their bright red shoulder patches—flit about the old bulrushes and cattails. Bluebills, the lesser scaup, float lazily in the open water, pausing on their northward migratory flight. Mallards—the green-headed drakes and the drab-brown hens—already have formed pairs. And they greet the warmer days with courtship flights overhead, a prelude to the more serious business of replenishing their own kind.

But down below, Mama has not changed much from her winter life style. The water remains cold; therefore she is yet sluggish. She does not wander far from the depths. Yet her special days are drawing near and she feels the swelling in her body. It is familiar—for she has sensed the spawning instincts many times before.

Mama is in her 18th season. They have been prosperous years. She weighs some 36 pounds and her muscular body stretches 52 inches—eight inches shy of five feet. She is one of the largest fish in her part of the bay. A 42-pounder lives on the next point, although they do not socialize much. Mama is not particularly a loner. She will occasionally join her own kind and stroll about the bay. But Mama is content. In Portage Bay, she has everything she needs. Ample spawning grounds and abundant forage fish, such as perch, whitefish and suckers. Deep-water hideaways, surrounded by vast fields of shallow pondweeds or potamogeton—convenient hunting grounds with places to wait in ambush for an unsuspecting meal. Oxygen, too, is rich amid the weed life, and the surrounding water stays cool and shaded in the heat of summer.

But a month now has passed since the ice disappeared, and April is well under way. The shallow bays have continued to warm. Mama is restless. The walleye and the northern pike already have followed their instincts. And the muskellunge is next in order—one of the last of the predator fish to spawn.

The bay already is alive with other fishes seeking the warmth of the sun-stroked waters. Meanwhile Mama has become increasingly nervous. She moves from her deep-water home and heads toward the shallow bay. The water temperature is nearing 50 degrees (F). While she earlier needed sufficient food to supply the demands of her body and the developing eggs, Mama now senses no hunger. And as she enters the warmed waters she pays scant attention to the many easy meals. The other fishes seem to sense her lack of interest and move boldly past as she cruises slowly along the bottom.

It is late afternoon when Mama first arrives in the very shallows where she, 18 years ago, first began life. Where she was left to fend for herself at birth, Mama now has company. Two younger males— smaller and about 36 inches in length—discover her presence and excitedly cruise to her side. Mama does not seem to mind her companions, although she does not particularly acknowledge that she is being followed.

Aimlessly and without effort, the trio of muskies cruises the shallows. Small perch dart ahead, surprised by the visiting giants. Mama moves into extremely shallow quarters, amid an isolated clump of bulrushes. The disturbance is greeted by a protesting male redwing. The brash blackbird slides down on a lone bulrush stem, swinging precariously in the afternoon breezes, and gawks at the underwater intruder.

With one flick of her giant tail, Mama could easily inhale her feathered protester. And in a different time and in a different mood, Mama would be tempted. But now she pays no heed to the squawking bird; she continues to explore the backwaters.

Her companions, the two males, follow her lead, occasionally darting ahead but soon swirling back to her. Mama ignores them for the most part, although she is well aware of why she has attracted a crowd.

On they cruise, swirling here, darting there, skimming through the gin-clear waters. At times they wander almost out of the water, showing their broad backs and reddish-pointed tails above the surface. Such little swimming room does not seem to matter. Nor do they seem to mind the clarity of their surroundings and their vulnerability to potential enemies.

Mama, however, shows more caution than her male partners. A sudden splash from a muskrat or the quick shadow of a gull overhead sends her darting toward the depths. The males follow, but they seem oblivious to any outside distractions.

The western sun is fading quickly when Mama glides into a wide flat shallow barely two feet deep. The bottom is layered with rotting vegetation—blackened bulrush stems and yellowed stalks and leaves of other aquatic plants. Mama pauses. It is dark but she has found what her instincts said she needed for her special task.

Her male companions seem to sense the proper timing. They begin to nudge Mama with their long snouts and move aggressively to her side. Mama swirls and glides away as the males become more amorous. But she does not go far. Nor does she discourage their advances.

Suddenly, the time is right. She has found the proper setting and her body is heavy with the burden of eggs. The spring winds have warmed nature's hatchery—the shallows—and Mama knows her time has come.

Her long sleek body—almost out of place in such skimpy water depths—begins to quiver over the weedy bottom. The first male reacts and quickly comes to her side. And in one graceful motion, the two fish roll on their sides, quivering. Their tails thrash effortlessly, almost in unison. And Mama lets go.

From her swollen anus, long strings of light, amber eggs—almost like pearls—spew out and swirl amid a milky cloud of milt released by the male.

The eggs—several thousand of them—scatter in every direction, swept away by the thrashing tails of the two spawning muskies. But the eggs do not travel far, nor is there a nest waiting. Each egg is sent off to fend for itself, to land where it lands. And even that landing can spell life or death. It is such a haphazard mating that only 30 percent or so of the eggs will be fertilized. And fertilized or not, some eggs will never develop, depending on where they fall. Still others will miss the matted vegetation and fall into unfriendly surroundings, such as sand or gravel. There, fungus may attack, destroying the egg long before it develops.

Mama of course does not know these things. As quickly as her mating started, it is finished. At least for the time being. Mama has more eggs to drop and she will repeat the spawning ritual several times through several days. And when her special calling is over—within a week's time—Mama will have dumped more than 200,000 potential muskies.

Nature has never believed in 100-percent success, of course. Nor does Mama care. She is exhausted after spawning and her eggs have barely settled when she quickly departs. Her male also leaves immediately, almost as if nothing happened. Unlike the largemouth bass, bullheads and several other fishes, neither Mama muskie nor her mates feels any parental responsibility. It's almost as if the muskie species—one that often exhibits the survival-of-the-fittest syndrome—must itself begin life under the same rigorous rule. If you are bent to devour other fishes through life, then the start of your own life must not be easy.

In a way Mama knew this lesson. Almost 18 years ago to the day Mama completed her spawning, she too had been one of those fragile muskie eggs—a small sphere of life, a mere three millimeters in diameter, tossed to the bottom of vast Portage Bay. By any measure, it is not only a miracle that Mama survived. It is amazing that anything survives.

Yet there were helpers—like the sun, which continued to warm the shallows and speed up nature's aquatic incubator. Within two weeks the water where Mama had spewed her eggs had warmed to 60 degrees (F). And the eggs—the lucky ones—were no longer completely transparent but contained one large "eye."

A day later the miracle of all miracles took place. The eggs were no more. Tucked here and there on stem and leaf on the lake floor, tiny quarter-inch muskie fry lay on the bottom. First lifeless, then squirting about only to settle down again. They are fragile creatures, vulnerable to both fish and insect prey. Vulnerable to almost any disturbance. The only thing that isn't a problem is food. For each young muskie fry still carries part of the egg, the yolk sac, which will serve for food in the first days after hatching. But the sac doesn't last long. And within five days after hatching the passive part of a muskie's life is over. The killer instinct begins, an instinct that will eventually eliminate tons of other fish life and shake the knees of human anglers. If the fry survives. Insect larvae and other micro-organisms are the muskies' first prey, followed closely by fierce cannibalism if the food supply should run short. Or even if it doesn't. Young muskies are quite willing to eat anything that looks alive and eatable—even each other.

Such a beginning is the law of the survival of the fittest in its strongest terms. For a young muskie must not only escape natural enemies, it must elude its own kind as well. Few wild things start life in such double jeopardy.

Lunge was one of the lucky ones. He hatched earlier than most of his brothers and sisters, and his predator instincts were well developed by the time life in the shallows became more dangerous. Within a month after hatching, Lunge was already several inches long. With a pencil-shaped body and black spots, Lunge also could easily hide amid the new plant growth, not only to protect himself but to lie in ambush for easy meals.

His mother, Mama, returned a couple of times, though Lunge did not know her. Nor was she interested in her young. Mama was hungry for bigger meals, last year's perch particularly. After spawning she had spent several weeks in deeper water until her body had healed. Her mates also were in the same territory, although they did not suffer from the spawning act and had resumed feeding long before.

But Lunge did not take any chances. At the first sight of Mama, Lunge darted for a dense stand of curly leaf pondweed. He had already had two close calls, one from a fish that looked much like Mama. A small northern pike had almost nabbed Lunge one day as he crossed an opening in the dense pondweed forest. Only a quick turn, an instant before the northern's attack had saved his life. And he knew it.

The other brush with death was still a mystery to Lunge. He had been floating lazily near the surface, alert to anything below, when he suddenly felt an explosion from above. A split second later Lunge sensed the pain of a puncture and the feeling of flying. A great blue heron, standing tall and quietly in the shallows, had eyed Lunge and took a wild stab. Herons seldom miss, but Lunge flipped at the right moment and slipped free of the heron's beak with but a slight cut.

Lunge knew nothing of his attacker, but he learned that danger can come from above and below. And it was a lesson that would prove valuable later.

Meanwhile the days passed and Lunge had become an aggressive flesh eater. From the time he was but one and one-half inches long his primary meals were at the expense of other fish. He learned to strike quickly and with deadly accuracy. In a snakelike rush, Lunge would grab an unsuspecting minnow from the side, first stunning his prey, then rotating its dazed body for the final head-first gulp.

Lunge also ate often. His body was growing rapidly. By winter, he would be almost eight-inches long. And size was important. For every inch meant fewer enemies. Though he was still fair game for any larger predator, Lunge no longer would be easy pickings for the dreaded mayfly larvae or the plump perch or the fiesty young largemouth bass.

Most of his brothers and sisters were not so fortunate, of course. Of the small minority of Mama's eggs that hatched, even most of those had already disappeared from one cause or another. And when winter finally arrived, Lunge had seen only five other young muskies his size. Nor had he seen much of Mama, for she had moved to another weed-bed several hundred yards away. Not that that bothered Lunge. There were other enemies, including different muskies, still roaming occasionally through his area. He remembered his lessons well, however, and rarely took chances.

And life went on. By the end of Lunge's second year he was already more than twelve-inches long. His spots had long disappeared and instead his silvery sides now were sliced with attractive vertical bar markings. His long snout already had that look of viciousness, complete with short but needle-sharp teeth. And he ate and ate some more.

There were additional hazards. In his second summer another northern pike—larger than the first pike that had attacked—made a mock charge at Lunge and could have inhaled him. Lunge had not expected the attack because the northern had not transmitted a feeding mood. Fortunately the northern was not serious. However, the big pike rushed upon Lunge as if to nail him, then suddenly changed course and sailed by within inches. Lunge didn't stay around to find out why.

Lunge did not know fear, however. Nor compassion. A narrow escape from the jaws of an enemy—bird, fish or reptile—was simply a matter of existence. He lived as his instincts dictated: hiding, running, hunting and generally seeking comfort and sanctuary. Brushes with death were commonplace and accepted. So, too, was his role as killer. He had to eat to live. And his instincts again required that his meals be alive. As such, Lunge did not know compassion for a perch any more than a wolf pack feels remorse about hamstringing a fawn. Like all predators, Lunge was an opportunist, alert for the unaware, the crippled, the easy mark. And as his own hunting skills became more finely tuned, the urge to satisfy his own hunger—while avoiding becoming a meal for some other meat eater—became easier with each growing day.

But in the spring of his third year Lunge experienced a new and strange adventure. And it all started one afternoon when Lunge, gliding through rather shallow water, spied a weak, struggling minnow that appeared to be almost suspended.

The dying antics of the injured minnow attracted Lunge's attention immediately, for his eyes were attuned for easy marks. The small minnow paused limply, then continued its slow, quivering motion. Lunge could not resist and in a quick flash he nailed the helpless minnow.

Lunge turned, then . . . he felt his whole body heaved sideways by a mysterious force. A sharp pain pierced his upper jaw. Lunge tried to turn back, to rush to the safety of the new vegetation, but he could not. And in his struggles, Lunge began to twist and turn violently against his unknown and unseen enemy. But his slender 20-inch body was no match. Then, suddenly, Lunge found himself in the air, swinging like a pendulum from his hooked jaw. He was frightened but not in much pain. His nervous system was not as finely developed as creatures higher in the animal kingdom. And so the hook that had penetrated his jaw was not particularly a problem, except, whatever it was, Lunge wanted to rid himself of his unseen captor.

It was then that Lunge saw his first fisherman, an elderly man, fishing simply for spring crappies.

"Well, by golly," the fisherman said to nobody. "Lookee here, a young muskie. You sure put up a scrap. Now just hold still a second and you'll be . . . oops."

Lunge flipped just at the right moment. The hook had been freed and his slimy body was too slippery to handle. And in seconds, Lunge found himself back in the lake. Surprised to be free, Lunge paused for a moment, regained his senses, then disappeared into the depths with one strong stroke of his tail.

Lunge still was unsure of what happened. In another year or two, the story might have been different. For Lunge would have been close to keeper size (30 inches) for some fishermen. Still, Lunge sensed a new danger from his adventure, the sight of man. And it would become a familiar sight in the remaining five years of Lunge's life. He would be hooked again—several times—but he also would eventually escape the barbed trebles. And he would see many more fishermen as he followed other tempting meals only to be led into the long shadow of a boat hull.

Lunge had a good memory, except it was awfully short. Time and again he would come dangerously close to inhaling another false meal. But time and again he also would make the right choice.

So what was really new? Lunge's life always had been a series of close calls and near misses. That he had one more adversary—the fisherman—was hardly worth noting.

He would survive a natural existence if his instincts warranted. If not, he might die early. In nature's world, not even muskies can ask for more.

6

In the Good Old Days

History did not record the details of man's discovery of the muskellunge. But it's worth a guess.

Undoubtedly a native American, standing on some river bank or paddling a birch-bark canoe, was the first to get a good look. And no doubt the Indian was confused by what he saw. Because everybody else has been since.

The muskie has more names than a con artist and more designs than a first-grade finger painting class. Even scientists—who normally ignore subjective conclusions—have not been able to pin down all the natural facts surrounding the muskellunge.

Consider the Latin name, *Esox masquinongy. Esox* is the equal of "pike." The equal of *masquinongy* is a little cloudy. In French, *mas* or *mis* means "large" and *kinonje* translates to "pike or fish."

It is generally agreed that the French version was lifted, possibly incorrectly, from the Cree Indians, who had a name, *mashk kinonge,* meaning "deformed or ugly pike." The original spelling is thought to be *maskinonge,* however, and the French translation comes out to be "long face," or *masque allongee.*

In Canada, the official accepted name is maskinonge, selected after

35

considerable controversy, because the fish was first known to exist in Canada and the various names stemmed from Canada's Cree, Ojibway, French, and French-Canadian dialects. But to further confuse the issue, early French settlers in Ohio called the muskie a *piconeau*.

But if you don't like those names you might try: mascalonge, muskalonge, muskallunge, jack, 'lunge, blue pike, etc. These and another 35 or so names probably complete the list for the watchamacallit. Or as outdoor writer Bill Vint once said, "There ought to be two more names, Old Mossback and Dirty S.O.B."

Finally, the accepted common name, among scientists and fishermen alike, is muskellunge. It's also agreed that the muskellunge (or musky or muskie—here we go again) is the largest member of the pike family of *Esocidae*, which includes the northern pike, chain pickerel and redfin or grass pickerel.

While you are entitled to ask, "Who cares about the muskie's relatives?" more than one angler has whooped with joy over landing what he thought was a muskie until somebody wiser told him it was a "nice northern." And worse, many fishermen have kept nice "northerns" that were indeed small muskies. In states where fish spearing is legal, such as Minnesota, many spearers—looking downward on the elongated shadow of a fish—often mistakenly stab muskies, which are illegal targets. As a result, lakes designated as prime muskie waters in Minnesota are closed to spearing.

Hook-and-line anglers really have no excuse for confusing the two species. The coloration of a muskie is best described as dark markings on a white or silvery background, whereas the northern pike has light marks or splotches on a dark body. There are of course differences in the head shape, though they may appear to be minor to the casual glance.

The muskie also has scales only on the upper half of its cheeks and gill cover, or opercle, whereas the northern pike's cheeks are fully scaled. The northern's gill cover is scaled in a fashion similar to the muskie's, however.

Perhaps the best field identification key is the sensory pore openings along each underside of the lower jaw. The muskie normally will have six to nine pores on each side, or an average total of 14. The northern pike usually has five or fewer, for an average total of 10.

Since the muskie and northern pike often share the same waters, and since fishing seasons, size limits, and creel limits usually are different, it is to the fisherman's advantage to recognize the differences between the two species.

Particularly since there is a third creature swimming in many parts of muskie-northern pike territory. That's the hybrid muskie, a cross between the true muskie and the northern pike. The hybrid, often called a tiger muskie (*Esox masquinongy x Esox lucius*) was first discovered in Wisconsin in 1937.

Again the untrained eye may mistake the hybrid for a true muskie or northern pike, although the hybrid has its own characteristics. Most obvious are the heavy dark bars, spots or stripes on the light-colored body—hence the popular "tiger" name. Even the cheeks and jaws are spotted. The hybrid's cheeks and jaws are partially scaled and the number of sensory pores under the lower jaw range from 11 to 13, counting both sides.

The hybrids forked tail is more rounded than a true muskie, but the differences are slight. And unless the tail patterns are side by side, an inexperienced angler might be hard pressed to note the differences. Again the sensory pores provide the best clue for proper identification.

Most state fish and wildlife agencies treat the hybrid and true muskie alike in regard to seasons and size limits. Historically, of course, the hybrid was an accident, a product of one of nature's interesting mistakes. But in recent years, the hybrid muskie has become the darling of state fisheries' managers. The fish—easily produced and raised in hatcheries—is fast growing and more conducive to fish-management goals. At the moment, that means muskie fishermen everywhere likely will be seeing more of the hybrid. Not that many anglers would object.

However, there are some die-hard enthusiasts who won't mention the hybrid and the true muskie in the same breath. Unless they fool and catch the real thing, they refuse to be satisfied. And they fear the increased emphasis on hybrid muskies will mean that populations of true muskies will suffer from both competition and lack of attention.

There are, however, good reasons to have active fish-management programs for both. For muskies of every description have suffered setbacks for the greater part of the last 200 years.

When Indians and Eskimos were the only human occupants of North America, the muskie originally was found only in the eastern portions of the continent: From Quebec eastward to Vermont, then south and west through New York, to the Tennessee River system, to parts of Ohio, and northwestward through the Great Lakes, Michigan, Wisconsin, Minnesota, to western Ontario and southeastern Manitoba.

Strangely, muskies were never present along the northern shores of Lake Superior. But the fish then reappeared westward in Rainy Lake and was abundant in Lake of the Woods and the English River system as far north as Sioux Lookout, Ontario.

The muskie was first described as a distinct species in 1824, although that contention was to be debated later on. Likewise, the muskie's origin is a subject of much speculation. However, it is generally agreed that the muskie originally was a saltwater fish that invaded freshwater river systems, such as the Mississippi River, and became isolated by glacial action. Later, the entrapped muskie was distributed by further glacial movements during the Ice Age. Indeed, fossil teeth belonging to muskies some 7,000 years ago have been found in Pleistocene deposits as far south as Oklahoma. Yet the muskie shows the least tolerance for salt or saline solutions of any freshwater fish. And while the muskie and the barracuda of saltwater fame have similar attributes, such as sharp dentures, the toothy critters are not related.

Controversy over the muskie's taxonomic features—its distinctions as a species—still has not ended, however. Even as late as 1924, Minnesota's fish superintendent, Thaddeus Surber, was convinced that the muskie was "nothing more than a local variety of the common pickerel or great northern pike (*Esox lucius*), which has, by long confinement to certain bodies of water, acquired certain peculiar characters in color and markings. . . ."

Since then, of course, ichthyologists have concluded that the muskie is a separate species, composed of three subspecies largely based on geographic distribution.

They are: the Great Lakes (*Esox masquinongy masquinongy*); the Ohio or Chautauqua (*Esox masquinongy ohioensis*) and Northern (*Esox masquinongy immaculatus*).

The Great Lakes muskie, often called the true or spotted muskie, is found generally within the Great Lakes basin, such as Lake St. Clair in Michigan.

The Ohio or Chautauqua is usually referred to as a barred muskie, notably in New York's Lake Chautauqua and southward into Ohio.

The northern muskie, also called the tiger, roams the waters of

Minnesota, Wisconsin, northern Ontario and portions of the upper peninsula of Michigan.

But while three subspecies most often are listed in official sources and muskie anglers continue to argue over the merits of each subspecies, further evidence suggests the subspecies listing is rather academic.

Noted outdoor writer Robert Page Lincoln, in a 1932 *Sports Afield* magazine article, questioned the need to separate the muskie into subspecies classifications. He wrote: "It is ridiculous in the face of present-day facts to separate the muskellunge because of varying marks and spottings. I have seen muskies come out of the Mantrap chain of lakes at Park Rapids, Minnesota—where the unspotted form, *immaculatus*, is supposed to be found so numerously—that have been heavily spotted or even barred."

He went on. "The fact is that a muskellunge striped like a tiger or a zebra does not fight any better necessarily than one that is spotted, blotched, immaculate or mud-colored."

Other early writers and taxonomic specialists also questioned the subspecies breakdown, noting that while the muskies may differ in coloration from region to region—or even within regions—there are no structural differences between the three muskie subspecies.

Minnesota's Al Lindner, founder of the In Fisherman Society and one of the most knowledgeable fishermen in the country, firmly believes the "muskie is a muskie."

In a 1976 essay on muskies in an *In Fisherman Report* (a fishing educational publication sent to members), Lindner investigated the subspecies question with Dr. E. J. Crossman, a University of Toronto professor of zoology and curator in charge of the Department of Ichthyology and Herpetology of the Royal Ontario Museum.

Crossman said there is only one kind of muskie and that it wears a variety of "coats." The color variation occurs simply because of local environment and other factors. Crossman indicated to Lindner that the muskie's basic features, not coloration, are the only safe criteria to use for subspecies classification. And those features, such as the number of fin rays and the arrangement and number of scales, do not vary sufficiently to warrent subspecies status.

Crossman pointed out that the young muskies—from all subspecies—cannot be distinguished. Until the young are about six inches long, they all have vertical dark bars on a light background. Later those markings change, apparently because of environmental factors in the water.

There the subject will rest. Besides, it is an old discussion and one not about to end soon. If a muskie is a muskie is a muskie, fishermen should take note. For you are seeking the same basic fish with the same basic habits and tendencies no matter where you happen to be fishing. In other words, muskie angling techniques popular in Wisconsin will undoubtedly work in Pennsylvania and vice versa. Meanwhile, let the fisheries scientists worry over the muskie's family tree.

For sure the early explorers and pioneers that settled over the muskie's original range weren't concerned with academic exercises. They were too busy hauling out muskies for food and sport.

According to historical records, most of the Indian tribes in muskie country did not rely on the fish as an important source of food. In fact, the muskie was consumed only after more preferred fish were not available. There is no indication that the muskie held any special god-like reputation among the various tribes. Quite possibly, due to the muskie's own nature, they never were an abundant source of food, compared to more prolific species. As a result the muskie likely was more difficult to catch in great quantities and, as such, was not worth the time and effort to the native Americans.

That distinction changed, however, with the arrival of white settlers. In that era of expansion and domination, starting in the 19th Century, nearly every resource was thought to be inexhaustible. Forests were cleared, prairies were plowed, rivers were mistreated, wildlife was eradicated—everything was exploited.

The muskie did not escape, either. Throughout its range, the muskie was subjected to commercial fishing pressures, starting in the 1800s. And it was a popular fish in the marketplace.

In Michigan in the 1880s, commercially netted muskies were bringing the highest prices throughout the Great Lakes and Lake St. Clair. At the time, the Michigan State Board of Fish Commissioners stated that the muskellunge is "very large and it appears not plentiful in any certain locality."

In Ohio, French settlers recorded catches of "piconeau" or muskies that "were stacked like cordwood along the shore." Union soldiers told of hundreds of muskies being caught in a single day at the mouth of Maumee Bay on Lake Erie.

Early sport fishermen in Minnesota and Wisconsin also sent messages back east of fantastic catches of muskies. In 1884, writer-angler C. H. Crane described his successes in the Hayward, Wisconsin, region: "On Monday we set out by team over a splendid forest road for Teal Lake, five miles away, where we put in a very enjoyable day with muscallunge . . . small but gamy, from two to fifteen pounds. The catch for five rods for the day was 78 fishes: weight 317 pounds. These were packed and sent to the 'heathen'—we did not know what else to do with them."

From early accounts in Minnesota's *Hubbard County Clipper*, the muskellunge, called the "sand lake trout," was hailed as "king of freshwater fish" in 1891. In 1889, a Colonel Harding—most famous for capturing Jefferson Davis at the end of the Civil War—led a fishing party to the Mantrap chain of lakes near Park Rapids, Minnesota, and told of catches totaling 300 muskies.

Other angler-explorers wrote glowing praises about the muskie itself: "It is the most perfect and beautiful fish that swims the freshwater and the flesh is simply delicious," wrote an Iowa fisherman, Dr. Kidly, in 1891.

"It is a large fish ranging from six to 30 pounds. The largest one caught by our party weighed 20 pounds. Several others weighed 15 and 17 pounds and 10 pounders are caught by the score. We consider a hundred of three, four and six pounders a good day's work. We have 1,500 pounds salted down."

In Canada's muskie waters similar exploitative ventures also were taking place. In the last 30 years of the 19th Century, thousands of pounds of muskies were commercially harvested in Quebec and Ontario. Ontario alone listed a commercial catch of muskies totaling more than 651,000 pounds in 1890. Ontario's Lake Simcoe in 1868 reportedly yielded some 229,050 pounds of muskies.

But it didn't last long. By 1901, the commercial netting of muskies was nearly a thing of the past in Ontario, largely because the original stock had been reduced from abundance to scarcity. Quebec stopped commercial netting in 1936. Yet elsewhere the mindless exploitation of muskies continued. In his book *Man Against Muskies*, Howard Levy recalled how market fishermen on New York's Lake Chautauqua took more than 900 pounds of muskies in one afternoon. Many fish were 30-pounders or better. There were no rules or regulations. However, by the end of the decade the muskie bonanza was depleted. In 1941, fishermen on Lake Chautauqua boated a mere 817 muskies during an entire season.

The future of the muskie looked bleak indeed. While the muskie's game-fish qualities were well recognized—and the fish became a tourist attraction starting early in the 1900s—the continuation of commercial marketing, crude sport fishing regulations and destruction or pollution of muskie waters prompted conservationists to predict the extinction of muskies.

In a March 1932 issue of *Sports Afield*, Robert Page Lincoln wrote: "Undoubtedly the Lake of the Woods section and a vast region north of it, chiefly the Lac Seul district, will be the last great stamping ground of the species (muskellunge) in North America.

"Fortunately," Page went on, "much of this region yet remains to be fished by anglers for the sport of it, therefore, it will produce potential fish for the next 75 years."

By the turn of the century, Wisconsin already had begun artificial propagation of muskies. In a 1901 publication of the American Fisheries Society publication, James Nevin wrote alarmingly:

"For many years since the wilderness of northern Wisconsin was opened by the railways and by lumbering operations: with the advent of the comforts and conveniences which the railroad takes into a new country, and the encroachment of the settler and summer hotel on the primitive banks of our northern lakes, the pursuit of the muskellunge has been constant and relentless. Its utter extermination has been well nigh accomplished in many of our lakes to which it is indigenous and nearly all of our waters have been cleared of this fish to such an extent that its future has become a matter of much concern to sportsmen, fish culturists and others interested in keeping our waters well-stocked with superior game fish."

New York started experimenting with muskie-rearing programs as early as 1890 on Chautauqua Lake and built one of the first muskie hatcheries in 1904.

Ontario collected muskie eggs in 1927 out of the Pigeon River and cultured them in a portable hatchery, marking Canada's entry into the muskie-raising business. Later, in 1940, the Deer Lake Hatchery, exclusively for muskie propagation, was constructed near Havelock, Ontario.

Of course as tourism, including tourist-fishermen, developed as an industry of its own, more states got into the muskie propagation business. The muskie already was an elusive and highly desired trophy. The mere mention of its presence attracted fishermen far and wide.

The community of Park Rapids, Minnesota, grew and prospered largely because of one single source, the muskie. And the local residents were well aware of the tourist dollars generated by muskie followers. Even in the early 1900s, the Park Rapids area was being promoted through advertising, showing pictures of large muskies and inviting people to "visit the area and plan an outing."

Of course the big muskie catches couldn't last forever. As the years passed it took more time to nab a muskie lunker and fewer were caught. Finally in 1914, Minnesota, too, took steps to begin raising muskies by collecting spawn from the Park Rapids area.

But as usual, the realization came too late that the muskie had been seriously depleted. In the summer of 1919 in Park Rapids, a big fish contest, sponsored by Earl Fuller to promote his hardware store, was won by a 22-pound muskie. Second was a 19-pounder. The days of the 30-pounders were over. Muskies of 15 to 20 pounds became acceptable. Still most anglers clung to the theory that "the big ones were still down there, but were too crafty to be caught."

Sadly they were mistaken.

The nets, the massive catches, the encroachment on muskie habitats had taken their toll all across the original range of the "water wolves." The heydays were over and there wasn't much left to shout about.

The muskie, of course, was just one victim. And not necessarily the most vital resource that was almost totally ransacked. Entire wilderness forests were leveled by timber barons; fur-bearers, such as the beaver, were trapped to near-extinction; the prairie and the prairie chicken both became endangered remnants. Many of the nation's waterways served as open sewers, carrying the waste of a growing industrialized nation. And what wasn't polluted was straightened, dammed or otherwise modified to pay the price of progress.

Of course the muskie suffered. Everything suffered. But the dawn of the 20th Century also marked a turning point in the country's attitude toward things natural. Under the leadership of men like Teddy Roosevelt, a new conservation conscience was born. Man learned to limit and control himself. The forests regenerated; the whitetailed deer returned. Wildernesses were preserved. Wildlife refuges protected the migrating waterfowl. Hatcheries resupplied the lakes and streams.

But more importantly, something called a sportsman developed. He was willing to pay for the privilege of hunting and fishing through the sale of licenses. He supported the levy of taxes on his specialized gear—his guns and ammo and rods and reels—to raise additional funds for the restoration and rejuvenation of the nation's fish and wildlife resources.

In addition, the new sportsman was willing to limit himself, to abide by rules and regulations, to participate under an unwritten code of fair pursuit. He learned that the quality of a man's experience was what counted, not quantity.

He discovered that a trophy whitetail buck was a worthy quarry, and deserving of respect in the way it was hunted. He found that any clod could waylay ducks on the water or swat a covey of quail in a fencerow. But it took experience and skills to outsmart the greenhead mallard over decoys or make a double on the covey rise.

And he found the muskie, a fish of excitement, size, and strength. A fish that possessed every requirement of the sport-seeking angler. And it was a fish that the sportsman-angler was willing to finance to have.

The good old days of muskie fishing had to be recaptured. It would take time, money and personal discipline. Waters had to be cleansed, spawning grounds preserved. Seasons would have to be set and limits obeyed. There were hatcheries to build and biologists to hire.

And a new fishing ethic had to be practiced: to fish for sport and trophy, not greed and meat. That meant "former trophies," the 15- to 20-pounders, had to be set free, released alive and healthy, to grow and live and strike again another day.

Each angler would have to do his part, to set goals and make his own contribution to the welfare and comeback of the mighty muskellunge.

That is where the muskie and the muskie fisherman are today. Progress is slow. The ranks of fishermen have increased steadily and not all have received the "fish for fun" gospel. Many states do not have successful muskie programs; others have tried and failed. And still others could have expanded muskie management except that other species have higher priority.

Nevertheless the comeback of the muskie is very real. It is working. And the good old days of muskie fishing may not be over but in the making.

7

Is There a Muskie in Your Future?

Let there be no doubt. Muskie fishing—the fanatical pursuit of the gamy muskellunge—is here to stay. An aware fishing citizenry wouldn't have it any other way. But what size is another question.

Skeptics still contend that the era of mammoth muskies—those 50- and 60-pound giants—is ancient history, that Art Lawton's 69-pound, 15-ounce world record is unbreakable. To prove their point, the skeptics will unfurl list after list of case histories that show gradual declines in size, numbers and frequency of muskie catches. And to cement their position, they'll demonstrate that fishing pressure is increasing by leaps and bounds. And that no muskie, no matter how smart, will be able to avoid being caught until it reaches world-record poundage. Of course there's always the chance, but the odds are slim or none, say the skeptics.

Undoubtedly the facts back up the conclusion, that while there will be fishing for muskies in the future, they will be smaller muskies.

But then the times have a way of changing. Thirty years ago, many fishermen and state fishery agencies concluded, with an armful of data, that the muskie was on the way out as an important sport fish.

Today, of course, nobody is making such claims. The struggle to restore the exploited populations of muskies is far from over. But if persistence is any virtue, the nation's muskie enthusiasts have it. And if it's possible at all, the muskie will thrive.

Consider the example set by Ellen Ramsell, a female muskie addict from Blaine, Minnesota. Her story of persistence and determination is but one isolated experience. But it shows the depth of dedication inherent to muskie followers.

It was on September 1 of 1974 that Mrs. Ramsell landed her first legal-sized muskellunge. She will always remember it well. She had already fished a total of 20 days that year before she hooked the 13-pounder. But she had fished for 25 years before that, averaging 24 days a year, without bagging a keeper. By her own calculation—fishing 25 years for 24 days a year for eight hours a day—she had made at least 500,000 to 800,000 casts for one legal muskie.

No matter how you slice it, you have to desire something madly to maintain that kind of faith. And muskie people have it. And why not? In June of 1975, Frank Weller of Chicago bagged a muskie a mere seven inches shorter than Lawton's 64½-inch world record. Although Weller's fish only weighed 43 pounds (only?), it was the longest muskie recorded in 12 years.

In recent years, two dedicated Minnesota muskie hunters, Dr. Jerry Jurgens and Chan "Doc" Cotton, each have caught 50-inch muskies that they have *released*.

Also in 1975, Wisconsin's Flambeau Lake produced a 51-pound giant for Gene Allen, of Kaukauna, Wisconsin, the largest muskie taken in the state in 22 years. And despite all the hoopla over the so-called golden years of muskie fishing, the records of the Freshwater Fishing Hall of Fame show that only 20 muskies over 50 pounds have been caught since 1919.

In other words, the really giant muskies apparently always have been rare. And the fact that some still are being caught, despite the very real problems of pollution, fishing pressure and so forth, means that there is hope, indeed. After all, if the early settlers had such fantastic muskie luck, why is the world record held by a muskie taken in 1957?

The truth is probably somewhere in between. There can be no doubt that the muskie was overfished, exploited and harassed throughout its original range. But history often appears greener than today's pastures, although the appearance may be misleading.

In more than a dozen trips to Wisconsin's Deer Lake, I can recall but one day when not a muskie was seen. Of course not every muskie spotted was caught. In fact, very few. And of those hooked, all but one dandy was under the 20-pound category, although 25- and 30-pounders were known to be swimming in the same waters. Granted those statistics do not smack of any era to remember. But do not forget that fishermen in the early 1900s also were hard pressed to find muskies over 20 pounds. And there was some doubt if anything heavier existed at all.

While it can be argued that 40-pounders have become rare in such famed waters as Leech Lake, Lake of the Woods, and Eagle Lake, a considerable number of 30-pounders still are being hauled out. That's more poundage than some areas could claim a half century ago.

Does this mean muskie fishing has improved? Yes. And does it mean that the future of muskies will also be one of improvement? It is possible.

The science and art of managing muskies, of restoring populations and of introducing new muskie waters has made great strides in recent decades.

Wisconsin undoubtedly has the most extensive and progressive muskie management program, involving dedicated biologists and managers, such as Leon Johnson. Johnson's fisheries research career has been almost totally occupied by muskies. He's examined everything from muskie limnological data to the speed of a muskie swimming.

The heart of Wisconsin's program, of course, involves the raising and stocking of muskies. Muskies originally were only found in about nine Wisconsin counties, not counting the river systems. Today that muskie range has more than tripled, with muskie fishing available in every county in the northern half of the state. And instead of some 450 muskie lakes and streams, Wisconsin now boasts of having about 700 bodies of water where muskies roam.

To maintain those waters, the state's Department of Natural Resources stocks some 20,000 pounds of muskies annually—each 10 to 12 inches in length to insure survival and supplement natural reproduction.

Muskie fishermen take an estimated 100,000 or more legal-sized muskies out of Wisconsin waters every year. Chasing muskies is a big business. In a random survey made in the late 1960s, Wisconsin found that, statewide, some 157,000 fishermen had made almost a million muskie fishing trips to catch 94,000 legal-sized (over 30 inches) muskies. And for every 100 legals hooked, some 190 undersized fish were caught and released. The successful anglers averaged nearly two legal muskies during the season. However, when all fishermen are included in the data, the number of muskies caught per angler drops to about .6 and the number of muskies per trip was .1.

While the thought of one tenth of a muskie per trip won't make a fisherman drool with envy, the extent of Wisconsin's commitment to maintain and increase its muskie fishing opportunities is encouraging and symbolic, perhaps, of the future.

Minnesota, Pennsylvania and Ohio also are examples of states that placed more emphasis on the muskie. In 1960, Pennsylvania started extending the range of muskies in the state's suitable waters. Shortly after 1940, the muskie had become rare in Ohio, with less than two dozen fish taken during the 1941 fishing season. Today hundreds of muskies are caught annually in Ohio.

On New York's famed Lake Chautauqua, the muskellunge population had been depressed to the point that by 1941 only 817 muskies were caught by sport fishermen. However, through research and management, and the construction of an extensive muskie-rearing station on the lake's western shore, the muskies in Chautauqua started making a comeback. By 1962, some 15,856 fishermen purchased special muskie fishing licenses and boated an estimated 7,720 muskies weighing a total of 43 tons for an average of about 11 pounds each. In 1955, Chautauqua gave up a 51-pound, 3-ounce trophy.

Increased muskie success has been reported in New York's Allegheny River as well as other muskie waters—mostly the result of stocking and management efforts.

Muskie fishing even returned to the nation's headquarters, Washington, D.C., when the Virginia Fish and Game Commission stocked Burke Lake, a mere 12 miles from the Pentagon.

Minnesota, also blessed with an abundance of natural muskie waters, has expanded its management efforts, though not to the level of Wisconsin. There are approximately 80 lakes and rivers in Minnesota with known muskie fishing. Of these, about 18 are designated as muskie waters, which means that winter spearing through the ice is prohibited. In addition, three lakes are used exclusively to maintain muskie brood stock for hatchery egg supplies. In recent years, Minnesota also has emphasized the stocking of 8- to 12-inch muskie yearlings rather than fry or fingerlings. Between 12,000 and 15,000 yearlings are stocked annually, both in natural muskie waters and in lakes where muskies historically were absent. Minnesota officials look at the muskie as a trophy fish exclusively. Hence some lakes are stocked with no hope of establishing natural populations but simply to provide opportunities to catch a trophy.

Iowa, Illinois and Missouri—three states with little or no historic muskie waters—have been the latest to introduce muskies into suitable waters with measurable success.

Iowa has managed to develop its own brood stock sources and thus expand its hatchery goals. Muskies were originally stocked in two lakes—Clear Lake and West Okoboji. In 1975, a reported 58 legal muskies were caught in West Okoboji. The first Iowa record, a 29½-pounder, came out of Clear Lake. But that record has since been broken two times, both in 1975, with a 32½-pounder and a 38-pounder out of West Okoboji. Iowa muskies also have been released in two reservoirs, Big Creek and Rathbun.

Another success story is unfolding on Missouri's Pomme de Terre Lake, where initial stockings have been producing good results, muskies in the 20-pound-and-up category. Although Missouri's suitable muskie waters are limited, the management plans for Pomme de Terre, if successful, could make it one of the top muskie lakes in the Midwest.

Illinois' entry into the muskie business still is in its infancy.

In 1955, Michigan's muskie picture, hammered by the same forces that eroded muskie populations everywhere, was looking quite dismal. Outside of Lake St. Clair, inland muskie fishing had declined drastically to the point where only 15 lakes remained that provided any muskie action.

That picture today is far brighter, however.

The Michigan Department of Natural Resources began experimenting with the hybrid muskie, the tiger, which resulted in an initial stocking of 17,000 tiger muskies of the 9-inch size in Hamlin Lake. It was not a cheap undertaking. Each 9-incher cost about $1.25 to hatch, raise and release.

However, the experiment appears to be quite successful. Early in 1975, a Michigan man speared a 32-pound tiger muskie to set a new Michigan tiger record. The fish came out of Hamlin Lake, which, prior to the stocking of muskies, was best known as a lake full of hammerhandle northern pike and stunted bluegills and bass. The 32-pounder and, later, a 26-pound tiger, have abruptly changed Hamlin's reputation, however. And Michigan officials have plans to expand their hybrid muskie program to include other inland lakes.

What about the hybrid or tiger muskie? A number of states are busily raising and stocking the colorful fish for good reason. While the hybrid, a cross between the true muskie and a northern pike, is usually sterile, the fish has many other attributes that appeal to fish managers and fishermen alike.

The hybrid, a shorter, more robust fish than the true muskie, grows considerably faster than its parents, sometimes reaching the legal 30-inch size within 30 months. The fast-growing true muskie takes four to five years to reach the same length, although either growth rate is spectacular when compared to most other game fish.

It is generally agreed—and the statistics indicate—that the hybrid also is an easier fish to catch, not that it doesn't fight. Hybrids are strong swimmers and have no qualms about aerial acrobatics once the hook is felt. However, fishermen surveys indicate that it takes an average of 20 hours of fishing per legal hybrid, whereas true muskies may hold out for 75 hours or more.

Fisheries managers look with favor on the hybrid, of course, for its rapid growth rate and hardiness under hatchery conditions. In addition, true muskies appear to have more specific requirements, regarding the type of environment preferred.

The rapid growth of hybrids helps ease the time between trophies at a time when more and more anglers are waiting. The angling public wants results. Many are not willing to wait the necessary years it takes to produce acceptable trophy-sized true muskies. And a hybrid may grow to be twice the weight of a true muskie, although stocked in the same waters at the same time.

The largest hybrid ever recorded, the world record, weighed 50 pounds, 4 ounces and was caught by Delores Ott Lapp in 1951 in Lac Vieux Desert, Wisconsin. That surely is an acceptable trophy to 99 percent of all muskie fishermen. But many observers feel that the hybrid's gullible nature, its tendency to be more easily caught, winter and summer, means that the number of really trophy-sized hybrids will always be uncommon. They argue that emphasis on the true muskie may require more patience but the true nature of muskie fishing—the quest for a trophy—will pay dividends in the long run.

In regard to fishing, the techniques that will land a true muskie will also fool a hybrid. Al Lindner of the In Fisherman and Ted Capra, one of Minnesota's noted muskie anglers, contend that the hybrid makes use of deeper water more often than the true muskie. And Wisconsin's Art Moraski, leader of the ARTS Fishing Research team, has concluded that hybrids do not feed at night, whereas true muskies may often exhibit voracious nocturnal feeding binges.

But otherwise there are more similarities than differences between the hybrid and the muskellunge. Yet some devoted muskie followers look at the hybrid as a "tourist fish"—a mass-produced, man-made trophy for a commercial venture, the tourism trade. As compared to the native, natural, historical muskellunge, which demands more time, more patience and perhaps more skill to be caught.

It's like the debate over Fords and Cadillacs. Both do the job but one does it nicer than the other. Yet there are disadvantages and advantages in owning either brand. Likewise, the debate over hybrids and true muskies.

Thirty years ago, state fish managers may never have considered the hybrid as a satisfactory replacement for the native muskie. But increased fishing crowds, the demand for more muskie fishing opportunity and the reduced levels of native populations forced some bold moves. Such as going with the hybrid stock.

And so far it appears the hybrid can and will do the job. But that doesn't mean the end of the true muskie. Quite possibly, the hybrid may take pressure away from the muskellunge itself. If that is a possibility, the purists may find that their beloved true muskie will have increased odds for living long enough to reach those dreamed-about sizes of 50 and 60 pounds.

Whatever, the rebuilding and expansion of muskie fishing in both the U.S. and Canada will require time, patience, manpower and money—and plenty of help from nature.

The spawning act of a wild, natural muskie is not the most successful venture. A 50-inch female may deposit some 150,000 to 250,000 eggs, but only about 30 percent of those will be fertile. In man's hatchery nearly 95 percent of those same eggs could be assured fertilization.

Also in the wild, by the time the fertilized eggs hatch, develop, grow and grow some more, scant few of the original egg count will reach adulthood. In fact, survival is so risky that very few muskie fry or fingerlings—raised and protected in artificial hatcheries for the first several weeks of life—continue to live once released in a natural environment.

As a result most states have dropped the stocking of fry or fingerling muskies. Although it costs more to keep the young muskies, stocking success is much greater if yearling muskies—nine to 12 inches long—are released. The greatest cost is supplying the food. It takes about four pounds of fish flesh to make one pound of muskie. By that time, the yearling has outgrown many potential enemies, leaving only predators such as bears, large birds, other muskies and, of course, man.

Not that predators are a muskie's only problems.

In exploring what makes good muskie waters, Wisconsin research biologist Leon Johnson found the definition to be complex. Some lakes—a mere two miles outside of the historic muskie range in Wisconsin—were unable to support muskie populations.

An unexpected die-off of muskie fry in the Woodruff Hatchery in 1963 provided a clue, however. Johnson found minute quantities of zinc in the hatchery's water supply, which later proved to be toxic to newly hatched fry.

Was zinc then responsible for the presence or absence of naturally produced muskies within a body of water? But what about other elements in the water that may reduce the toxicity of zinc? Those complex questions still are largely unanswered.

Johnson also discovered that naturally spawned muskellunge eggs were quite susceptible to low water temperature. In water 42 to 50 degrees (F) most muskie eggs simply died without developing. However, when new eggs were placed in the same lake, after the water temperature had reached 55 to 60 degrees (F), a normal hatch occurred.

Since no one can do much about the weather or the presence of zinc, you may wonder why such information is valuable to a muskie fisherman. Granted such research won't help you land a lunker. At least not directly. But muskie fishermen, of all people, should understand that muskie management can be a complex task. That it is not simply a matter of dumping fish into a lake. That to act without knowledge is a waste of your fishing license money. And that waste only further postpones what fish managers and fishermen both want—healthy, viable muskie fisheries.

Despite being armed with the best information possible, the stocking of muskies is still a long shot. Consider Wisconsin's famed muskie lake, Court Oreilles. A 1972 study of the lake's muskie population showed that the muskie numbers ranged from 210 to 338 with an average of 244, an all-time low. That's 244 muskies living in 5,000 acres of water. Yet Court Oreilles had been stocked with muskies every year since 1933 with the exception of four years, 1966-1970.

What happened to those fish? Many things. An estimated 15 to 25 percent of the legal-sized muskies in a lake die every year of natural causes, such as parasitism and disease. Not the least of a muskie's problems is a cancerous tumor, called Lymphosarcoma.

The tumor usually starts on the side of the fish and may spread to the fins, head and gums. Eventually death may result.

There are of course such things as accidents. Muskies do get hit by outboard motor props. Muskies can choke on food or suffer a host of other pitfalls.

But the disappearance of most muskies—from fingerling size to giants—is rather easily traced to predators, ranging from fish to man. Once hybrid muskies reach legal size, for example, an estimated 35 to 45 percent of the adult mortality is at the hands of fishermen.

Perhaps the most vivid picture of what happens to muskies is provided by another Johnson study on Wisconsin's Court Oreilles, the 5,000-acre muskie lake near Hayward.

For three years the lake was annually stocked with 1,000 muskies of five to 12 inches, each marked with a fin clip. Later, the fish were re-marked whenever one was captured during spawn-taking operations or by electro-shocking.

The resulting life table of what happens to 1,000 muskies over the years is quite revealing. Almost 90 percent of the stocked muskies were gone, disappeared, within the first year.

The death rate then abruptly slows until the muskies reach an age of five years. Then 29 of the remaining 94 muskies are suddenly eliminated. That's fishing pressure. And by the 18th year, fishermen, predators, accidents and you name it have combined to eliminate all but two of the original 1,000 muskies.

Other studies have indicated that not all muskie stockings are eliminated at such a fast pace, however. In a study of 10 other Wisconsin lakes, Johnson found that the survival of muskie fingerlings ranged from 25 to 96 percent with an average of between 35 and 40 percent. The reason for the various survival rates was not readily ap-

The Court Oreilles Population

Age (Years)	Number Alive at Start of Year	Number Dying During Interval
½-1	1,000	886
1-2	114	5
2-3	109	5
3-4	104	5
4-5	99	5
5-6	94	29
6-7	65	13
7-8	52	16
8-9	36	10
9-10	26	7
10-11	19	5
11-12	14	1
12-13	13	4
13-14	9	2
14-15	7	2
15-16	5	3
16-17	2	0
17-18	2	0

Based on three (1955-1957) year classes; Johnson, 1975 *Wis. Cons. Bull.* 40(5):20-21.

parent, although it was noted that lakes with more aquatic vegetation per acre also had the higher muskie survival.

Other factors of lesser importance were length of fingerlings stocked, water temperature of the lake and the length of predators in the lake.

Most of the actual early losses of muskies were caused by predation. The newly stocked fingerlings disperse rather rapidly, swimming the lake shoreline and exposing themselves to a vast number of potential enemies. Johnson, for example, found that on the 5,000-acre Court Oreilles, the newly stocked muskies would distribute themselves around the lake's 28.9 miles of shoreline in about seven days.

Fishermen-caused muskie mortality becomes more important later, of course. For example, an Ohio study on the Leesville Reservoir indicated that a large percentage of the total annual mortality of muskies was directly attributable to fishermen. Approximately two out of every three muskies dying annually in the reservoir were dead because they were caught.

Yet despite such a high catch rate, a small percentage of muskies, less than two percent, escaped to reach sizes of 35 pounds or better.

There is then hope that the muskie in your future will be big enough for the wall. And how big is that? That's a question that every angler must answer for himself. But regardless of whether your idea of a muskie trophy is 15, 30, or 70 pounds, you, the muskie fisherman, are in the best position to make your own luck.

No, muskie fishermen cannot babysit every yearling muskie or muzzle every hungry predator. For the most part, the natural mortality must be accepted as the price of doing business.

It is known, however, that the effects of predation can be minimized if the young muskies have the suitable habitat—the weedbeds—in which to hide and escape from enemies. But weedbeds have a way of disappearing, largely because of man-caused changes. Shoreline developments, such as housing projects, marinas, beaches and so forth, are often proposed with little concern for the "weeds" that line the shallows. Many riparian owners look at aquatic vegetation as a nuisance, an unsightly blight on their lake view. As a result, unknown miles of weedy shorelines have been destroyed, largely for very selfish reasons.

But in addition, a lake's fisheries potential is also crippled. For aquatic vegetation is nearly as important to muskies—and almost all fish life—as is the water. The weedy bays, the shoreline patches, the cabbage or pondweed beds serve many uses. They are spawning grounds and later nurseries for nearly every fish species. They are hideouts and hunting grounds for both the prey and the predator. They are, in fact, an important key to thriving fisheries, particularly muskies.

More importantly, the concerned muskie fisherman can do his part to insure the future of the proper habitat. Bodies of public waters should be under the jurisdiction of state resource agencies. And those agencies should have the appropriate rules and regulations concerning developments on or over the waters. Of all water users, fishermen have the most to lose if such controls do not exist. And if they do not exist, get involved in the legal processes of your state, usually the legislature, to provide for the protection of public waters.

Be aware of proposed developments alongside any fishing lake. What do the plans include? Will extensive dredging take place? How much of the shoreline or aquatic vegetation will be disturbed? Again, make it a point to be informed and alert about projects that may needlessly reduce or destroy the future of the fishing sport.

Lastly, the fisherman must also learn not to be his own worst enemy. For example, trolling can be very destructive to weedbeds. And many trollers thoughtlessly cruise back and forth over weedy muskie haunts, tearing up huge chunks of fish habitat. While the troller may cuss the weeds, he is hurting the muskie and himself.

Of course it is impossible to troll and not nab some vegetation. But the trolling fisherman should take great pains to avoid passing over thick patches. In addition, he should use a lure or plug, such as bucktails, that trolls rather shallow, skirting the top of weedbeds. Using the proper lure will minimize the damage to the aquatic plants without minimizing your chances of fooling a muskie.

Without proper habitat, no amount of muskie fishing regulations or muskie stocking will save the muskie and the sport. Let there be no doubt.

But also do not doubt that the muskie enthusiast is in the best position to protect that habitat. It just means getting involved. With your resource departments, your legislatures, your fishing clubs. And of course it requires your own personal commitment.

Therein lies the future of the muskie and muskie fishing.

It is that simple.

Part III

Of Madness

8

The Eternal Search

A man's got to believe in something. I believe I'll go fishing.
—Thoreau

Muskies are where you find them.

Catching one is not easy but neither is it difficult. The muskies' own history shows that fishermen en masse can put a considerable dent in a muskie population. The fish is curious and aggressive. And both characteristics tend to put hooks in the mouths of muskies.

Yet the muskie remains an elusive trophy to the individual angler. Collectively, fishermen are an influence on population, but alone, each angler finds that he may be powerless against the muskie's whims. He cannot predict a muskie's behavior, nor can he consistently put a muskie in the boat. And no matter if the angler has landed one or a hundred muskies, the next one seldom is any easier.

Some fishermen know. For they indeed have gone seasons between legal muskies or they have spent years looking for number one. It shouldn't be that way. The muskie is only a fish. It is confined to water. Its wants and desires are controlled by the same forces that affect other fishlife. Still, the muskie remains clouded in mystique and myths—not because the muskie is anything supernatural but because strange things happen when you're holding a muskie rod over muskie waters.

59

John Lundquist, a member of Minnesota's Muskies, Inc., had been fishing for muskies an entire week on Leech Lake. He had had zero luck. It was time to head home. Lundquist started his outboard and took off for the campground to start packing the camping gear. On the way across the lake, he decided to stop for one last cast in a known muskie area. He made the cast. His first legal muskie of the year, a 21-pounder, nailed the hooks.

Marty Olson, another Muskies, Inc., member, experienced the same frustration. He had fished hard for 13½ hours one day for nothing. Last cast. Bang! Olson hauled in a dandy, 36 pounds, 10 ounces.

But that's muskie fishing. As it's said, anything can happen . . . and it usually does. And the eternal search goes on. In the 1974 Muskies Inc., fishing contest for members, some 283 muskies were entered by 102 members. Yet 56 of the members entered only one fish. The other 46 members had accounted for 80 percent of the muskies caught. And ten of those fishermen were responsible for 40 percent of the total entries.

Is it no wonder the mystery over muskies lingers on?

Obviously those figures show that many fishermen try to nab a muskie but only a few connect. But the few successful anglers are extremely successful. Therein lies an important lesson: It is possible to become a better muskie fisherman, to learn more techniques, to bag more muskies more often.

Then there is luck. Even the most successful muskie fishermen will tell you that lady luck has a lot to say about heroes or bums in muskie fishing. Of course there is an element of luck in all fishing. A good bass fisherman may distinguish himself by finding the right bass-catching pattern on a particular day. If he does, he'll catch more bass than the angler in the next boat. He was lucky, but he also showed skill and talent in finding the proper technique or pattern.

There are patterns in muskie fishing although not nearly as many. Most muskie fishermen do one of two things: they cast or they troll. The selection of lures is rather universal; that is, there are few "secret" weapons. In other words, there are not many techniques that the good muskie fisherman uses that the poor muskie fisherman doesn't know about. Thus enter lady luck.

However, don't get the wrong impression. Lady luck is mentioned only because the foolish fisherman ignores luck as a factor. Luck does play a part in everything from fishing to throwing 60-yard touchdown passes. But if you expect to fish by luck for trophy muskies, your den will be far from cluttered.

Art Lawton was "lucky" to catch the world's record but Art Lawton also had put in his time. He did a lot of things right in trolling the St. Lawrence.

Chan "Doc" Cotton was "lucky" to boat 108 legal-sized muskies in one season in Minnesota in 1974. But Doc Cotton paid the price. He worked hard and learned from every experience.

Homer LeBlanc has waylayed some 3,500 muskies in a long career of fishing Lake St. Clair in Michigan. But Homer LeBlanc also was an inventive man who devised trolling techniques and invented a special trolling lure, the Swim Whiz.

Al Lindner of the In Fisherman Society and Spence Petros of *Fishing Facts* magazine landed and released 18 muskies in 13 hours on Wisconsin's Deer Lake a couple of years ago. And before that, Lindner and his brother Ron nabbed 28 muskies in six days of fishing on another Wisconsin lake. How? Again by hard work and by using their previous experience and knowledge to pick muskie lakes that are ripe. Sure, they happened to hit the ripe lake at the right time (there's some luck involved). But if you can't recognize a muskie hotspot, how can you ever expect to be there at the proper moment? That's too much to ask of luck alone.

As you can see, there's no great mystery about the eternal search. Muskies aren't easy, but they're not impossible, either. And with any luck at all, a fisherman willing to work and learn should be able to land a legal muskie in a matter of days. For sure, it shouldn't take years, unless you're absolutely snakebitten. Of course if you're talking about hanging a 30- or 40- or 50- or 60-pounder on the wall, you'd better plan on taking your time. Because without luck, you'll need it.

Muskies by their nature are not abundant fish. An excellent muskie lake may harbor a mere two muskies per acre. And the average muskie water probably contains less than one keeper per acre. Population densities such as these already make the search difficult at best. Keep in mind that the muskies per acre is an average figure. In any specific lake, there may be acres upon acres with no muskies present, except for an occasional passer-by. Muskies are not always evenly distributed because the habitat is not always uniform. Theoretically, one bay or one point could, in fact, harbor the total muskie population in a lake. Consider Rainy Lake in Ontario. Rainy is a huge sprawling body with a myriad of bays and islands that all tend to look alike. Rainy's walleyes, smallmouth bass and northern pike seemingly are scattered throughout. But if you're after muskies, there is only one bay—Red Gut Bay—where you might reasonably stand a chance of being successful. Red Gut Bay, by itself, is huge, however.

My first adventure there was with Carl Oetting, a spirited white-haired muskie addict who guided and managed a resort in the bay. Carl of course knew of known muskie haunts. But he also avoided many weedy bays that looked inviting to a first-time visitor.

"Oh, that's a good spot for northerns," he'd say, "but I've never found a muskie there."

You don't really know until you've tried. But Carl already had tried. The point is: it is not enough to simply travel to a muskie lake and expect action, unless the lake is small enough to fish completely. Such lakes are unusual. Many of the well-known muskie lakes—Minnesota's Leech Lake, Wisconsin's Chippewa Flowage, New York's Chautauqua, Michigan's Lake St. Clair, Ontario's Eagle Lake, the St. Lawrence River—are extremely big. And you could cast or troll all day and not be within a mile of the nearest muskie.

There are ways to reduce those odds, however.

Most states will provide a list of their muskie fishing waters. Chambers of Commerce usually are most willing to give details on the muskie hotspots within their areas. Other sources—such as outdoor magazines, newspaper articles, and even books—also will help get you pointed in the right direction.

Many bait and tackle dealers, marina managers or even dock bums will be willing to part with more specific muskie fishing information when asked.

Local muskie enthusiasts are still another source of information. Some hometown experts fully enjoy their reputations and feel flattered that you would seek their advice. It may even be good advice. But don't expect any muskie fisherman to provide specific directions. He is not about to divulge his hard-earned knowledge to any stranger. He is not going to say, "Fish 10 yards in front of the crooked oak tree and cast to your right." Or if he does, you'd better question the directions. Nevertheless, you'll pick up various tidbits from the local addicts to make it worth the time. At the very least, the expert may suggest a certain bay or shoreline. And if you've done your homework, you shouldn't need further guidance.

Of course the surest way of finding muskie haunts on a strange lake is to hire a guide. You'll spend more money but you'll also spend less time on the shore gathering advice and more time fishing. Do not think that hiring a guide is some kind of insult to your own ingenuity.

Many top-notch muskie fishermen—when visiting foreign muskie waters—will pay for a guided tour of the hotspots. They're not hiring a teacher or a babysitter. It's just that experienced muskie fishermen know they can't possibly seek out the most productive fishing grounds in a day or even a week, particularly on large waters. So why waste time searching, not knowing if you're even close, when a guide in one day can show you enough potential areas to keep any muskie fisherman busy for the remainder of his visit? Studies also show you'll do better with a guide.

Select your guide with some care, however. Again, ask around. Usually the legitimate, reputable guide is well-known in an area and you'll hear his name mentioned by more than one source. If not, you rightly ought to question his credentials. If you're still not sure, examine his boat and gear. A well-established guide will be properly outfitted with safe, modern equipment. He'll have references.

Be aware of the dock loafer who hangs around waiting for "tourists" who are willing to spend a few bucks for a guide. The bum will gladly volunteer, offering a great line of "you shoulda been here yesterday" stories to impress his vulnerable clients.

Assuming you've found a reliable source, it is wise to inquire about the guide's preferred fishing method. If he specializes in trolling while you prefer to cast for muskies, the differences may cause problems. The guide of course should respect your wishes, but then you'll be losing the advantage of having a guide doing his own thing. He may know less about the proper approach to casting for muskies than you do if he always trolls.

Thus, it is best to find a guide who shares your tastes in fishing. He'll be a better guide and you'll have a better time.

There's still another way of getting the inside scoop on muskie techniques and places-to-go. Join a muskie fishing club, if one is available. If not, you might consider starting a chapter or club. Muskie addicts come in all sizes and shapes and they're scattered throughout the country. But if there is anything a muskie addict likes second to fishing, it's discussing the ins and outs of the disease with others with the same illness.

Most clubs are formed for the reason of exchanging ideas and information and for protecting their own interests: muskies. So, you'll feel comfortable about asking questions and, otherwise, adding information to improve your own skills. What's more, you'll be able to meet and hear the the the best muskie fishermen in the area. And most of what you'll be told will be free of gibberish. No fisherman who has earned respect as a muskie expert will risk his reputation by delivering a message of hogwash. Within a club there are too many knowledgeable fishermen who could easily challenge the expert's word.

But aside from learning more about your favorite sport, most clubs have projects that also provide the opportunity to get involved, to accomplish constructive programs that will lead to better muskie fishing in the future. That alone is reason enough to join with fellow muskie anglers.

Partial list of Muskie Clubs

Muskies, Incorporated (MI)*
1708 UniversityAve.
St. Paul, Minnesota 55104

MI Chapters: Fargo-Moorhead
                94 Woodcrest Drive
                Fargo, North Dakota 58102

                Muskie Hunters of Illinois
                446 North Cedar
                Galesburg, Illinois 61401

                Pomme de Terre Muskie Club of Missouri
                Pittsburg, Missouri 65724

                First Wisconsin Chapter
                525 Woodward Ave.
                Chippewa Falls, Wisconsin 54729

Bill Hoeft's Muskie Club
932 South Third Ave.
Wausau, Wisconsin 54401

Blackhawk Muskie Association
Box 664
Janesville, Wisconsin 53545

Iowa Great Lakes Muskie Club
Box 148
Royal, Iowa 53157

Husky Musky Club of West Virginia
3511 Randolph Drive
Parkersburg, West Virginia 26101

Kentucky Silver Muskie Club
6804 Mariposa Drive
Louisville, Kentucky 40214

Michigan-Ontario Muskie Association
23323 Liberty
St. Clair Shores, Michigan 48080

Muskellunge Club of Wisconsin
3451 North 95th St.
Milwaukee, Wisconsin 53222

Wisconsin Muskies Limited
Box 502
Waukesha, Wisconsin 53186

Pennsylvania Muskie Society
701 Yardley Commons
Yardley, Pennsylvania 19067

Project Illini
5612 West 127th St.
Palos Heights, Illinois 60463

Ohio Huskie Muskie Club
Building C, Fountain Square
Columbus, Ohio 43224

Muskies, Inc., is a parent organization for several state chapters totaling more than 2,500 members in 27 states and Canada. Muskies, Inc., owns and operates its own muskie hatchery and rearing facility at Battle Lake, Minnesota.

Still, the eternal search must be faced alone. You can share a boat with dozens of muskie authorities and you'll start thinking, "Hey, I'm pretty good." That is, until you face up to the fact that the fellow in the other end of the boat is the source of your talent. There is only one way to become an accomplished fisherman of muskies, of bass, of trout, of anything. And that's by doing your own thing.

I know. As the outdoor writer for the Minneapolis *Tribune*, I am in the fortunate position of being able to fish with many experts—professionals, if you will. Of course I couldn't help but learn. And boy, did I ever catch a lot of fish when in the company of such fine "guides." But I also realized who was running the boat, who was choosing the spot, who was recommending the bait or lure. I was merely a passenger; the pilot was in charge. It dawned on me that if I was to become a better fisherman, I'd have to take over the responsibilities. While I used what I learned from the experts, it had to be applied alone with no outside coaching.

The weaning period was not easy. My early successes were dismal. But I was learning. Yet, any success was purely by my own doing and that was sufficient reward.

Searching for muskies requires no less. Again, in my early muskie fishing days I was almost totally dependent on a partner. Any beginner is. Nobody is born with muskie fishing prowess. Such a skill is not passed through genes. But I was eager and content to learn until, armed with enough weapons, it became necessary to fight my own battle with the elusive fish.

Most of my teachers still are better muskie fishermen. I do not profess to be an expert, nor do they. No one knows all there is to know about muskie fishing—or any kind of fishing. That's the beauty of the sport. The thinking fisherman will have a question on his lips on the day he makes his last cast on earth.

But the good muskie fishermen have one common ingredient, one trait that separates the haves from the have-nots. That's confidence.

It's said that there is one sure way of identifying a muskie fisherman. He never carries a stringer in his tackle box because he never expects to catch anything.

Not so. At least among the experts. Chan "Doc" Cotton and I were partners one day on Minnesota's Leech Lake. Doc had hardly fished 15 minutes when he began wondering out loud why he hadn't yet had a strike. That's confidence. He knew muskies could be caught and he knew he could catch them. After all, in the summer of 1974 he landed 108 legal-sized muskies, all witnessed. But Doc also had confidence in where he was fishing. He knew the lure at the end of his line would fool a muskie. He knew his rod, reel, line and terminal leader would do the job. All combined, he fully expected to nail a muskie; he had reason to fish with confidence. Every cast was important, receiving his full attention. In every part of the lake he fished, he expected action. There was no lost motion. He fished with confidence.

Granted the value of confidence is rather abstract. It is not something you can buy at the local sporting goods store. It is not a technique or method of fishing. Nor is confidence something that you just decide to have. You can't say, "I'm going to fish with confidence today" and expect to do so. Confidence stems from a variety of sources, a culmination of past experiences and mental attitude. It's the fruit of positive thinking. But confidence also is very elusive.

The consistent winners in the national bass tournaments will admit that confidence is their number-one ally. When they have it, they win, but it is not always there. For unknown reasons, confidence comes and goes. It is not something that once you have it, you'll have it forever.

But confidence is forever worth striving for. It is the sole key to consistency as a muskie fisherman. When you fish with confidence, the feeling permeates every motion. It affects how you fish, where you fish and what you do with a lure.

This is no exaggeration. Confidence is a valuable asset in nearly every endeavor. But its importance has special meaning when the sport is muskie fishing.

You are already looking for a needle in a haystack. Muskies are at the top of the food chain and, as such, are not an abundant species. Add to that the muskie's personality—unpredictable, stubborn, downright antagonistic. On some days you can fish the most crowded muskie hangouts in a lake and see or catch absolutely nothing.

With those two strikes, you'll need all the confidence you can muster just to keep plugging away.

The eternal search continues, only now you're more confident. So let's get to the meat of that search: the trophy, the big one, the giant muskie suitable for framing. You won't find many meat fishermen in the world of muskie fishing. Most of them have starved to death. For the average angler, muskies are too few and far between to count on as a source of winter food supply. And the experts—those who waylay muskies consistently—usually are obsessed with size, not quantity.

Not that the meat of a muskie isn't excellent dinner fare. Contrary to popular opinion, the muskie is indeed a fine eating fish with firm, white flesh.

There are, however, other reasons why the muskie is seldom thought of as a meat fish. The fisherman who accidentally hauls in a muskie (probably thinking it's a northern pike) will usually hang it on a stringer for a trip to the frying pan. But the hard-core muskie fisherman knows he has too much at stake to arbitrarily fillet every muskie that's brought to the boat. Because every sub-trophy muskie removed from a lake means that much more time before the replacement reaches trophy size.

Fortunately, the muskie is one of the fastest growing freshwater fishes. At four or five years of age a muskie may reach 30 inches, twice as long as a bass or walleye of the same age. The female muskies grow the fastest and live the longest. Males seldom live more than eight to 12 years, whereas females have been known to survive to the ripe old age of 30 years or more.

Yet muskies' growth rates vary considerably from lake to lake, from region to region, for a number of reasons: water temperature, food supplies, habitat and so forth. Knowing the growth rates is of value to fisheries managers in planning a stocking schedule, for instance. But such information also deserves consideration by the muskie fisherman in search of trophy waters.

Consider the following chart:

The blank spaces in the table do not mean that big muskies are not found in those waters. Larger fish merely happened to be missing in the sample when the chart was made.

However, Porter made note of the unusually heavy weights of Lake of the Woods muskies and the stockiness of 40- to 46-inch muskies from Wisconsin's Chippewa Flowage. While the variances may be due to the sampling procedure, both bodies of water are well known for producing trophies. Those reputations appear to be supported in the table.

Porter also took the table one step further by estimating the length of an imaginary 70-pounder, if such a fish had been present in the sampled lakes and rivers. His results are interesting. Since muskies tend to be more fat than long in the Chippewa Flowage, a 70-pounder might only be 56 inches long. Whereas the fast-growing Lake of the Woods muskie might stretch 73 inches long. The average for all areas for a 70-pound giant was 64 inches.

When compared to some of the known giant muskies, Porter's estimate of an imaginary 70-pounder is apparently quite accurate. Cal Johnson's 1949 world record out of Wisconsin's Court Oreilles was 67 pounds, 8 ounces with a length of 60¼ inches; Louie Spray's record out of the Chippewa Flowage, also in 1949, measured 63½ inches for its 69 pounds, 11 ounces. Art Lawton's current world-record muskie, 69 pounds, 15 ounces, measured 64½ inches in length.

Poundage is the single measure of a muskie in the record books, of course. But what about the age of a muskie and its relative size?

Wisconsin's top muskie biologist, Leon Johnson, and other fish managers have noted that lakes or rivers that produce muskies of about average growth rate also produce more longer-lived muskies. Rapid

A Comparison of Muskie Weights and Lengths*

Weight in Pounds

Size Inches	Piedmont Lake Ohio	Penn. Average	Chautauqua N.Y.	Lake St. Clair	Mich. Average	Wis. Average	Chippewa Flowage Wis.	St. Lawrence River N.Y.	Lake of the Woods
30	6.8	6.6	6.1	6.0	5.8	7.6	5.3	5.6	9.1
31	7.6	7.3	6.7	6.7	6.5	8.3	6.1	6.2	9.8
32	8.5	8.1	7.4	7.4	7.3	9.1	7.0	6.9	10.6
33	9.5	8.9	8.2	8.1	8.1	9.9	7.9	7.6	11.3
34	10.6	9.8	9.0	8.9	8.9	10.7	8.9	8.4	12.1
35	11.8	10.7	9.8	9.8	9.9	11.6	10.1	9.3	13.0
36	13.1	11.7	10.8	10.7	10.9	12.5	11.3	10.2	13.8
37	14.4	12.7	11.7	11.6	12.0	13.4	12.7	11.2	14.7
38	15.9	13.8	12.7	12.6	13.1	14.5	14.1	12.2	15.7
39	17.5	14.9	13.8	13.7	14.3	15.5	15.7	13.3	16.6
40	19.1	16.2	15.0	14.8	15.7	16.6	17.5	14.4	17.6
41	20.9	17.4	16.2	16.0	17.0	17.7	19.3	15.7	18.6
42	22.8	18.8	17.4	17.2	18.5	18.9	21.3	16.9	19.7
43	24.9	20.2	18.8	18.5	20.1	20.2	23.5	18.3	20.8
44	27.0	21.7	20.2	19.9	21.7	21.5	25.8	19.8	21.9
45	29.3	23.3	21.7	21.3	23.5	22.8	28.3	21.3	23.1
46	31.7	24.9	23.2	22.8	25.3	24.2		22.9	24.3
47	34.3	26.6	24.8	24.4	27.3	25.7		24.6	25.5
48		28.4	26.5	26.1	29.4	27.2		26.3	
49		30.3	28.3	27.8	31.5	28.7		28.2	
50		32.3	30.2	29.6	33.8	30.3		30.1	
51		34.3	32.1	31.5	36.2	32.0		32.2	
52		36.4		33.4	38.7	33.7			
53		38.6		35.5	41.3	35.5			
54					44.1	37.3			
55					46.9	39.2			

*compiled by Larry Porter, of Minnesota's Muskies, Inc.

growth in a fish, particularly if it's excessive, will usually reduce its life span. In the case of muskies, a rapid-growing muskie simply may burn out and die before it reaches trophy size.

Again because of differences in a body of water, such as food supply, competition, temperature and so forth, the age of a muskie and its size will vary.

Consider the following chart:

Comparison of Age and Length

	Location		
Age	Lake of the Woods	St. Lawrence River	Northern Wisconsin
5	— ins.	33.4 ins.	28.2 ins.
6	28.0	34.5	31.3
7	32.0	36.7	33.8
8	31.1	39.7	36.4
9	34.9	43.8	38.0
10	33.8	46.8	39.7
11	37.1	46.3	41.2
12	37.4	45.5	43.1
13	40.2	—	44.4
14	37.3	—	45.6

For a composite look at a muskie's size, poundage and probable age, Wisconsin's Johnson came up with the following chart for muskies out of Wisconsin's northern lakes. Keep in mind the figures may vary from region to region, although the differences will be minimal.

Length, Weight and Age Averages

If your muskie was this long—	The average weight would be about—	The average age would be—
8 ins.	.2 lbs.	½ yrs.
10	.3	1
18	1.0	2
25	3.5	3
28	5.0	4
30	7.0	5
33	9.5	6

36	13.0	7
38	15.0	8
41	20.0	9
45	27.0	10
52	42.0 and up	14-19

Also keep in mind that the figures are averages. The length of a muskie at a particular age may vary as much as 5 or 6 inches, longer or shorter. Fisheries biologists determine the age of muskies by counting annular or growth rings on a scale, much like counting the rings of a freshly cut tree.

The age of most scaled fishes is determined in the same manner. However, a microscope is necessary, as well as considerable skill in reading the scales.

An easier method, one the fisherman can do at home, it to separate the vertebrae of the backbone of a cooked fish and count the circles on the ends. Neither method is foolproof, however. The vertebrae aging technique also means the fish must be killed first. For the muskie fisherman curious about the age, it is more practical to measure the fish and compare its length against the age, such as indicated in the preceding charts. Or you may carefully remove a few scale samples and ask a biologist friend to read the scales. In that way, you can satisfy your curiosity about the age and still release the muskie unharmed.

Very simply, the more you know about the muskie the better you will guide your own way to better muskie fishing. Surely it is not necessary to memorize any charts. But you're after a trophy and trophies have to grow. It can't hurt to know where that happens and how long it takes. And don't forget, a trophy is a very special fish in many other ways. For it survived where thousands, and possibly millions, did not.

And where might that be?

If chasing a trophy is the eternal search, then *where* is the eternal question. Again research has shown that most of the muskies seen by anglers are from 30 to 36 inches long; they weigh from eight to 36 pounds and they range in age from three to 15 years old.

On New York's Lake Chautauqua, despite the intense management, despite the amazing success and comeback of the muskie, the average angler can only hope to catch a muskie that is 34 inches long, weighing 10 pounds. That is definitely better than nothing—which is about what Chautauqua had to offer in the late 1930s. But 10-pounders are hardly trophies, although that's the average and there are larger muskies to stumble upon.

What about Wisconsin, home of six former world records? In Vilas County, records have been kept of the catches during the county's "Muskie Marathon Contest." For a 12-year period, the results have been most interesting. From 1964 to 1975, a total of 16,160 muskies were entered for an average of 1,346 a year. The lunker sizes ranged from 38 to 51 pounds. But the average for all fish entered was only 12.2 pounds. Judging from the entries, the chance of catching a muskie over 20 pounds was about 1 in 10; a 30-pounder was 1 in 20; and on until the odds for a 40-pound-plus fish were 1 in 400. What's more, only a few lakes out of the 200 or so muskie lakes were consistently producing the largest fish.

Muskies, Incorporated, the largest collection and organization of muskie fishermen in the country, has a contest every year for its members. So—how do they fare in pursuit of the muskie? In 1975, a total of 632 muskies were entered, of which 536 were released and 96 were kept. The average length of the released muskies was slightly over 35 inches or slightly over 10 pounds. The fish that were kept for various reasons averaged almost 20 pounds, undoubtedly an indication that the fish kept were considered to be trophy size. Again remember the 20-pound figure is the average.

But is a 20-pounder a trophy? That depends on who catches it. If that's the first "decent" fish caught by a beginning muskie angler, it most likely will be hauled to the dock. On the other hand, the angler who already has caught, and possibly kept, say, a 25- or 30-pounder, really has no use for a 20-pounder outside of the thrill of waylaying a good muskie. And don't kid yourself, a 20-pounder is a good muskie, not only by today's standards but by yesteryear's as well.

But also—as we've examined the road to the eternal search—there is no doubt that the really giant muskies (those mammoth species that are longer than canoe paddles and older than teenagers) are hard to come by. In fact, some skeptics believe that the days of muskies over 60 pounds are gone already. That's a fairly safe assumption. Lawton's world record, taken in 1957, has held up longer than any previous record going back to the early 1900s. Some of the best known muskie fishermen of today—learned anglers who travel far and wide throughout muskie country—cannot boast of anything much over 40 pounds. And it's logical to assume that if more giants truly lived, at least one would be subdued sooner or later.

The entire discussion, however, is rather academic. Nobody knows, one way or the other, the status of 60-pound muskies. But all muskie fishermen realize that the fish is capable of reaching such colossal sizes in any body of water under the right conditions. And someday—out of some forgotten weedbed or sunken island or weathered boat dock—a new world record may come forth.

Therein lies the muskie fisherman's eternal hope. It may be a long shot, but then so is muskie fishing. Nor is there evidence that the seeker of record or near-record largemouth bass or walleyes or northern pike has a brighter outlook. In fact, the opposite may be true. Muskie addicts are an intense but select minority among the nation's angling corps. Far greater numbers of anglers pursue the bass, the northern pike, the crappie, the trout. Therefore if fishing pressure is the primary reason lunkers are scarce, the muskie yet may be the best bet. What's more, it is not a crime to be optimistic.

Larry Ramsell, a muskie fanatic and world records secretary for the Freshwater Fishing Hall of Fame, agrees that trophy hunting has declined over the years, but he's sure the game isn't over.

In compiling muskie records for the Freshwater Fishing Hall of Fame (a nonprofit organization based in Hayward, Wisconsin), Ramsell noticed several trends, particularly in regard to where the lunkers came from.

His conclusion: Big water produces big muskies.

He also noted that the lakes that historically harbored giant muskies are still doing so. That is, there has been little change, outside of the newer bodies where muskies have been introduced. Of course, the size of a lake or river is not the only criterion. A big lake with an inadequate muskie food supply may not even support a muskie population. So you can't select the largest lake on a map and say, "That's where the lunkers live."

However, Ramsell's point is: Among the known suitable muskie waters, the larger the better.

Here's why:

Consider the long and wide St. Lawrence River. It is the home of the world record. However, the river also has produced more muskies over 60 pounds (10) than any other body of water, according to the records of *Field and Stream* magazine. Granted, the lunker production from the St. Lawrence was taken by only four fishermen: world record holder Art Lawton and his wife, Ruth, and Len Hartman and his wife, Betty. Nevertheless, let the record stand. Since 1911, when *Field and Stream* first started maintaining records, the St. Lawrence has also yielded 13 muskies over 40 pounds and 13 over 50 pounds, in addition to the 10 over 60 pounds. Keep in mind that the listing represents only those muskies recorded by *Field and Stream*. Undoubtedly there were many more, say 40-pounders, that never made the record books.

The sprawling Lake of the Woods, located on the Minnesota-Ontario-Manitoba borders, is the second most mentioned hotspot in the *Field and Stream* records. Through 1972, Lake of the Woods gave up some 56 muskies over 40 pounds and 17 over 50 pounds, but none over 60. The largest Lake of the Woods muskie is 58 pounds, 4 ounces. Lake of the Woods also has held three former world records.

Ontario's Eagle Lake ranks third as trophy waters with 16 muskies over 40 pounds, five over 50 and two above the 60-pound mark. One of Eagle Lake's 60-pounders taken in 1939 was a world record; the other, 61 pounds, 9 ounces, still is the Ontario record. According to Ramsell, Eagle Lake did not appear on the *Field and Stream* listings until 1937. Up until 1933, there were no roads to the lake.

The remainder of Ramsell's selected trophy waters, listed by state or province, is as follows:

Lake	Over 40 Pounds	Over 50 Pounds	Over 60 Pounds
Wisconsin			
Chippewa Flowage	13	3	1*
Grindstone Lake	2	2*	-
Lac Court Oreilles	2	-	2*
Minoqua-Tomahawk	6	1	-
Lac Vieux Desert	9	1	-
North Twin	3	1	-
Butternut	5	-	-
Flambeau Flowage	5	-	-
Minnesota			
Leech Lake	5	1	-
Little Winnibigoshish	2	1	-

New York			
Lake Chautauqua	4	-	-
Michigan			
Lake St. Clair	3	2	1**
Canada			
Pipestone	3	2	-
Dryberry	3	1	-
French River	5	-	-
Cape Vincent	3	1	-
Rainy Lake	4	-	-

* 1 world record
** 2 world records

Keep in mind that the 40-, 50- and 60-pounders listed for each lake are only those received by *Field and Stream*. By no means does the listing represent each and every trophy taken. However, these lakes were the most frequently mentioned and therefore deserve special attention in every muskie fisherman's eternal search.

Of course there's a myriad of other spots where giants are supposed to swim. For example, there's "Old Bismarck," which lives by Elephant Rock on Red Gut Bay in Rainy Lake. Old Bismarck is so named because she's a muskie version of a ship, some 8 feet long, say the natives. Or was it 9 feet? She's been hooked at least twice and seen more often than that—always within the shadow of Elephant Rock, which looks like an elephant lying on its side in shallow water.

Old Bismarck is said to go 100 pounds. And the last time she was hooked, an old Indian guide testified that she cruised around for the better part of an hour attached to the treble hooks. But she tired of that game, glided next to the boat and charged off in a powerful rush that simply straightened her wire captors.

It was on a quiet, moonlit evening on Red Gut Bay—with the wilderness loons singing their mournful songs—when Carl Oetting first told me the story about old Bismarck.

"But she hasn't been seen now for about two years. Not that I've heard about," he added.

The next day Carl and I roamed about Red Gut Bay, tossing muskie plugs in several of his favorite haunts. We'd had a muskie or two on but none were landed.

"You want to try Elephant Rock?" Carl asked. He didn't have to wait for an answer.

The waters surrounding the giant, two-humped chunk of granite were glassy silent on that windless morning. Carl cut the outboard several hundred feet away from the rock and we quietly glided within casting range.

The surrounding wilderness was like a tomb. Not a gull or loon peeped.

Nervously, I reared back on my muskie rod and heaved a surface plug within inches of Elephant Rock. The ripples scattered. I twitched the plug. Nothing happened. I twitched it again. The ripples formed . . . and all hell broke loose.

A colossal wall of water erupted. The plug disappeared. Water flew in all directions. I leaned back quickly on the rod. I was stunned. Was this Old Bismarck?

I never found out. Whatever it was, the damned thing missed the plug.

Nor do I know if there really is such a fish as Old Bismarck. Doesn't matter. When a simple surface strike near a chunk of rock can make electric butterflies in a man's stomach, when it can jiggle the knees and stop the heart, then there *is* an Old Bismarck in Red Gut Bay. What's more, there are other Old Bismarcks scattered throughout the muskie waters of North America.

That's what the eternal search is all about, if only in the minds of muskie men.

9

Keep Your Line Wet

You can if you will.
—author unknown

There are only a few truisms about muskie fishing.

Muskies have been caught in water depths from 12 inches to 12 fathoms. They'll clobber a motionless surface plug or inhale a bottom-bouncing jig. And no doubt there's been a muskie taken in, every hour of the day and night, on everything from unpainted chunks of metal to artfully tied streamers to gobs of nightcrawlers.

In short, muskies are catchable anytime, anywhere, anyhow—with varying degrees of success, of course.

But there's one absolute, unbreakable rule: You'll never catch anything with a dry plug.

That's guaranteed. But that's why muskie fishing separates the men from the boys (with all due respect to female muskie addicts). Pure and simple, muskie fishing is hard work if you're casting, and trolling can be tedious. The casual angler is not able to do either very long without becoming dispirited and probably bored.

Of course muskies have been caught on the first cast in the first hour of the first day. One group of Minneapolis fishermen once visited a muskie lake in Ontario and landed 45 legal muskies in a day. And not one of the fishermen had ever caught a legal muskie before. But such incidents are the exceptions to the rule. The average fisherman on

Michigan's Lake St. Clair can expect to catch one muskie for every 225 hours of fishing time. On Michigan's inland lakes the time requirement is 80 hours, except where hybrid muskies are involved. Then the estimate is 20 hard hours.

On New York's famed Lake Chautauqua, fishermen haul out some 6,000 legal muskies a year. If you put them all in a wheelbarrow, those fish would weigh some 30 tons. But the average man with a fishing pole will spend 70 hours on Chautauqua before he nabs one 10-pounder.

Chauncy Hubbard, who's fished muskies for more than half a century, kept records of his exploits in the Hayward, Wisconsin, area. After counting for 37 years, Hubbard concluded that it takes 600 casts a day to maintain an average of one muskie in the boat.

An Ohio study figured that it takes 100 hours of fishing per muskie.

Suffice it to say, you can expect to spend some time. Even the most knowledgeable muskie fishermen confess that they'll spend 10 to 30 hours on the water for every muskie brought to the boat.

Granted, such a rate of productivity is enough to make a fisherman turn to golf. Yet there is something missing in those muskies-per-hour figures. There has to be. Otherwise the sport of muskie fishing would have died long ago from lack of interest. And that's not happening. If anything, the muskie is more popular today than ever before. Why? Because a guy likes to fish for nothing for 100 hours? No. Because the raw data doesn't tell the complete story. No one counts the exciting follows—those heart-throbbing moments when a muskie trails inches behind your hidden hooks right to the gunwales of your boat. No one counts the missed strikes—those vicious boils in the vicinity of your plug. No one counts the spirit of the hunt, the quest for something to admire and remember forever.

These are the things that motivate a muskie fisherman. And that is why he is able to defy the law of diminishing returns, to continue when others have quit. A dedicated muskie fisherman will fish 10 or more hours a day without a break. And those that do pause, say for lunch, may even switch to a surface plug and heave it out on the water just to sit while the sandwiches are being devoured. You never know. All it takes is for the right muskie to come along who's looking for an easy meal. Remember: you can't catch anything with a dry plug.

Then where do you get it wet?

For some reason the beginning muskie fisherman thinks that

muskies hang out in some mysterious cove that only old, weathered guides and lucky fishermen find; that the spot to catch a muskie must have a little bit of this and a little bit of that. What "this" and "that" are, he's not sure.

I know. I used to think that you could find muskies only in some super spot, some special corner on a lake that was impossible to find without knowing somebody or asking God.

Of course the whole assumption is absurd. The muskie, despite its many attributes, is really just a glorified northern pike. Whereas northerns normally are associated with aquatic vegetation, so too is the muskie.

The typical muskellunge lake is marked by having extensive fields of emergent and submergent vegetation, usually one of the pondweeds of the genus *Potamogeton*. Experienced muskie fishermen refer to the pondweed as cabbage, pike weed, redtops, lunge weed, or muskie weed.

It is an important plant to learn to identify. For whenever pondweed is present, the muskie will almost always be nearby, either directly in the bed of pondweeds, or on the edges (both inside and outside edges of the bed) or outside of the weedbed in a deep-water drop-off.

Depending on the clarity of the water, pondweeds may grow as deep as 20 or more feet. Although the weedbeds tend to grow to within several feet or less of the surface, they can be difficult to find at times.

Polaroid glasses are a valuable aid in "seeing below the surface," and most muskie anglers wear them. The glasses help in locating submerged vegetation, shallow bars or boating hazards. But Polaroids also enable a fisherman to spot muskies that might be cruising near the surface or following the lure. Personally, I wouldn't go fishing without such important eye wear. Good quality sunglasses make eye-care sense whenever you're on the water for any length of time. But equally important, the Polaroids are another "weapon" in your favor, particularly when casting.

The curious muskie routinely has the habit of trailing a lure, possibly trying to decide if he should eat the darned thing or not. The fisherman who doesn't see the follow, who stops retrieving his lure at the boat or who merely lifts the plug out of the water, is missing an excellent opportunity to hook a muskie. Not to mention the simple fun and excitement of seeing the fish.

More than once I've credited my prescription Polaroids for any of the muskie action that may have occurred in a day's outing. One late afternoon on Lake of the Woods, my fishing partner, Ray Ostrom, and I weren't exactly setting the world of muskie fishing on fire. In fact we had fished a good hour or two with not so much as a strike. Of course we kept trying. Then it happened. A 20-pounder, following deep below my lure, arrived at the boat. I yelled at Ray. While I attempted to keep the lure moving, the muskie acted as if he no longer was interested. Ray took the hint and threw a gold Rapala in the muskie's direction. The new easy meal was too much for the muskie. In an instant, the silvery fish had lashed into the Rapala. But before Ray could react the 20-pounder was out of the water and the lure went flying back to the boat. Okay, officially no fish was caught. But without the Polaroids, I probably wouldn't have seen the muskie follow and Ray wouldn't have been able to see what was happening, either. And instead of having an uneventful day, we had shared a bit of knee-shaking excitement.

Of course some lakes with muskies do not have an overabundance of pondweed. And since the muskie can't pack up and move to another lake, the fish must make use of what's there—lily pads, bulrushes, coontail, cattails, or downed timber.

In lakes along the Canadian Shield, such as Rainy, Eagle and Lake of the Woods, you'll find muskies present with no apparent abundance of pondweed. Or, at the most, sparse stands. But you will find the muskies "close to something." Such as huge, partially emerged boulders with deep water nearby. Quite often the boulder (or rock island, if you will) will mark the drop-off. And shallow water will be on the boulder's backside, along with emergent vegetation and some pondweed. Such a combination gives the muskie everything he needs: shallow hunting grounds with abundant forage fish, underwater boulder fields in which to hide and stalk, and deep water in which to escape.

Sunken islands and long underwater points—each adequately adorned with vegetation, depending on the depths—are the two major types of structure. (A shallow weedy bay, of course, has its own structure or something different in the form of openings, channels within the weedbed.)

And in most muskie waters, there will be muskies on both of those structure types, islands and points. Sunken islands (and some underwater points) may be difficult to find, however, without the aid of an up-to-date hydrographic map or an electronic depth sounder or both. By now, most fishermen are familiar with the electronic sounders or sonars and understand the value of such fishing aids. Suffice it to say, if you're not acquainted with these devices then make it a point to remedy the situation. While the sounders often have brand names, such as fish locators, fish finders and so forth, their real value is in locating the drop-off, points, bars, sunken islands and other muskie haunts. Once you learn to read the sounders, you'll know when you're over those all-important underwater weedbeds. The flasher or graph model sounders will even indicate if the bottom is mud, sand, rock or boulders.

Oh yes, the sounders will indeed show fish. But in the case of muskie fishing, that particular luxury is of limited value. By the time a muskie appears on the flasher or graph, it's probably been spooked by your presence.

Research so far indicates that muskies travel at relatively shallow depths, not much more than five feet. And while the muskie is built for sudden bursts of speed, the fish normally travels at an average of about one mile per hour.

Since the muskie also spends a great deal of time on the edge of or within weedbeds, your sounder also will be useless in such a setting as a means of pinpointing a muskie. Thus, the best advice is to concentrate on locating the proper muskie waters, the weedline drop-offs, the humps or points, the sunken islands, the cabbage or pondweed beds. Of course it's thrilling to spot a big fish with a sounder, so go ahead and keep watching. But if you're thinking that electronic wizardry will pinpoint a muskie for your wall, forget it. I've seen lake trout fishermen on Lake Superior troll all day through hundreds of "graphed fish" and never get a strike. And those fish are easy to see because they suspend. Muskies are known to suspend at times but under most conditions the muskie is an "object fish." That is, the muskie will be associated with some underwater object, such as weedbeds, drop-offs, islands and the like.

If the use of electronic gadgets is ethically displeasing, remember that such devices are not necessary. You can find many good muskie hangouts with the use of the hydrographic maps. It may just take longer, that's all. And you can use your eyes. Many times the surrounding terrain of a lake will give you obvious hints about what contours lie beneath the water.

A long sloping ridge or point that appears to end at shore more than likely continues underwater. A sheer bluff at the water's edge usually means a sheer bluff below. Boulders or sand on the shore may indicate what's on the adjacent lake bottom. Quite often the emergent vegetation—that which you can see—will show you exactly where an underwater bar or point starts and ends.

The skilled muskie hunter learns to use everything at his disposal. If he happens to use a depth sounder, that doesn't mean he forgets the value of his eyes. Your eyes can read the water the fastest. It's only when your eyes can't see that the sounders or maps come in handy.

Now let's put it all together. You've accepted the fact that muskie fishing may involve hard work, long hours and patience in return for moments and memories that will last a lifetime. And you're ready to keep the plug wet.

You've chosen a lake with a history of muskie fishing, based on reliable sources. You've launched the boat, the gas tanks are full and you're ready to drown a set of treble hooks.

What next?

Even the experts, when possible, will consult with the locals—the bait dealer, the cabin owner, the resort operator, other fishermen. Any tidbit of information can be of value. "Yah, there been a few muskies taken on the west shore"—that's a start. Take a look at the west shore on the hydrographic map. What's there? Large shallow flats, a sharp drop, small underwater humps? Is the west shore rather nondescript, hardly muskie-looking water? Maybe you got a bum steer? But you might fish the area later after trying what appear to be more likely-looking muskie haunts.

But suppose there is no one around. You're on your own. Roll out the map and open your eyes. No map? Okay, suppose you don't have a map or a depth sounder. Finding the muskie haunts would be easier, of course, with both of those tools. But the mental processes are unchanged. Maps and machines can't do your thinking for you.

Hop in the boat. What you need now is a good look at as much of the lake as possible. Look for points. Where's the longest point on the lake—or what appears to be the longest? If you're on a midsummer muskie trip, that's as good as any place to start fishing. Cast or troll along both sides, including the very tip. If you can see some kind of aquatic vegetation around the point, so much the better. If the longest point doesn't produce, try some of the other points. You can't be far off the track of a muskie.

Can you see any above-water islands? Try them, no matter what size, from a hump of rocks to a full-fledged tree-covered oasis. Again cast or troll the island's entire circumference, working water depths that appear to be shallow or deep. If you're not sure, tie a heavy sinker to a chunk of monofilament line and check the depth. After you've done that enough times, you won't forget your map the next time and you'll probably run out to purchase a depth sounder.

Nothing yet? Cruise the shoreline. Can you see a weedline, the place where the shallow growing pondweeds give way to the dark depths? No weedline? That's probably dead water, no fish. If a weedline is present, by all means start fishing again.

Two points on a lake usually mean there's a bay in between, of course. And bays are notorious aquatic gardens and muskie hideaways. Some bays are better than others, as you might expect. But your best indicator is again the presence of pondweed, assuming it grows in the lake of your choice.

Are there any inlets or outlets, such as rivers coming or going? These are often ideal spots, not only where the river enters or leaves but also the shoreline in the same vicinity.

If this was a muskie trip in early summer or into the fall season, you'd probably do well by starting in the bays first, followed by the inlets or outlets. Muskies spawn in the bays; the lake water warms first in the shallows and the muskie's food is most abundant there. The outlets and inlets offer the muskie some of the same comforts.

Muskies tend to spend most of the summer associated with deep water (at least 15 feet or more), moving into nearby shallows with the urge to feed, if food is unavailable at greater depths. But in the fall, muskies tend to spend more time in the bays again, particularly in lakes with tullibees or ciscoes—ideal bite-sized food for the muskie. The tullibees and ciscoes move in to spawn in the fall and the muskies follow. By the way, that's why the famed muskie lure, the Cisco Kid, is so named.

Without a map or depth sounder, you of course are unable to find the other potential hotspots on the lake, the sunken islands and underwater reefs, the underwater points and saddles.

But you also should have discovered that adventuring into the unknown, in this case a strange lake, does not have to be some kind of a mysterious guessing game. You can see enough with your eyes to catch a muskie. And you will if you keep your plug wet.

So when's the best time to do that?

Any old arm-weary muskie junkie will tell you that the best time to fish muskies is whenever you can. For sure, you can't nail a muskie by just thinking about it. And again muskies have been caught from one extreme to the other, from the humid heat of August to the ice-cracking days of January.

If you're a muskie addict any time is a good time. In 1974, when Chan "Doc" Cotton of Walker, Minnesota, caught an unbelievable 108 legal muskies, he spent 124 days on the water from early June to mid-November. There was an inch of snow on the ground when he quit with the 108th fish.

Strangely, Cotton's least productive fishing time was in August, a month normally considered to be good. There is no particular reason for his poor August luck, except that he spent some 10 days in pursuit of muskies in Canada, hit unsettled weather, and caught nothing. His best action, by far, started in mid-September and continued into mid-November. July also was fair, producing some 21 muskies. Out of 124 days on the water, 64 days were for naught. Nevertheless, Cotton averaged one legal muskie for every 7.6 hours of fishing, a catch rate that may be a modern-day record.

Generally, muskies are thought of as a midsummer fish, the ideal quarry for the vacation season—July 4th to Labor Day. And most catch records back up this assumption. A breakdown of the muskies caught per month during 12 years of Wisconsin's Vilas County Muskie Marathon shows:

Muskies Caught Per Month
(16,160 fish)

May	10%
June	22%
July	22%
August	22%
September	14%
October	8%
November	2%

The muskies caught by members of Muskies, Inc., over two seasons,

1974 and 1975, demonstrated a similar monthly catch rate, based on more than 1,000 fish:

May	4%
June	8%
July	17%
August	24%
September	21%
October	18%
November	8%

Do muskies hit better in, say, July, or are there simply more muskie hunters out then? The answer is a little bit of both. Muskies are not notorious as an active cold-water fish. For example, very few true muskies are taken by ice fishermen.

Muskies feed most actively in water ranging from 68 to 78 degrees (F). Although the fish can tolerate water temperatures as high as 90 degrees, they show signs of stress in such warm water and their feeding rate drops. The same is true in cold water. When the temperatures fall much below 60 degrees, muskies also consume fewer meals. At the muskies' most active temperature, 68 to 78, the body metabolism is functioning best. As a result, muskies may require a meal or more a day, sometimes amounting to 10 percent of their body weight. Such food demands are drastically reduced in colder waters. Since a muskie is cold-blooded, it is, in fact, "comfortable" in any reasonable water temperature. Aside from fatal temperature extremes, the only time a muskie "requires" a particular temperature is for spawning.

In that sense, it follows that the more active a muskie feeds the more vulnerable it becomes to the fisherman's bait. Therefore, more muskies should be caught in midsummer, regardless of the size of the fishing crowds.

Of course there are other factors that again cloud the question. The muskies' food supply also is most abundant in summer, a supply in direct competition with the angler. A hungry muskie normally doesn't have to hunt long or far in such abundance, thereby reducing the fisherman's chances of attracting a strike. The only advantage under such circumstances is the muskie's own predator instincts. Being a born opportunist, a muskie may not resist the temptation to smash an easy mark (the lure) even though the fish really is not hungry. Of course with so many muskie anglers out and about in the summer, someone is bound to be in the right place at the right time.

The apparent low muskie fishing success rate through late spring may be the result of different factors, however. After spawning, the female muskie often retreats into a period of inactivity while her tired and sore body regains strength. Such inactivity may last for two weeks or more. However, the smaller males often go on a feeding binge immediately after spawning. On Wisconsin's Deer Lake, for example, the spring crappie fishermen, using small minnows, are harassed by muskies on the prowl. Most, however, are small males and under the 30-inch legal size. Occasionally a keeper muskie will be taken, much to the surprise of the crappie fisherman, but it is not common.

Trophy-conscious muskie anglers often ignore the spring fishing as well, despite the relative ease of catching small muskies. There's always an outside chance for a trophy, of course. But most muskie fishermen—even the addicts—will wait until June before starting their annual muskie marathon. In fact, in Ontario it is illegal to pursue muskies any earlier since the season normally doesn't open until mid-June.

However, muskie fishermen—being creatures of habit—may be their own worst enemies during the early-season period. It is tempting and natural to fish those areas in a lake that led to success the previous season. That's a good idea if your timing is right.

But the shoreline weedbed that harbored muskies last July may be completely evacuated in June. Not understanding the muskie's seasonal movements, the angler concludes that early-season fishing is lousy. And the word spreads and fewer fishermen try.

In some lakes and in some seasons, the growth and development of weedbeds, or weedline breaks on sunken islands and deep-water shorelines may be delayed. Since there is little vegetation to "hold" a muskie, you won't find it there. The muskie needs both food and cover. Thus, when the vegetative cover is missing or still inadequate, the muskie will resort to deep water as a cover substitute.

In early spring the vegetative cover first starts growing in the shallow bays where the warmer water and sunlight are adequate. And for a short period of time, many muskies will frequent such bays. But in that transition period—between the muskie's spawning, shallow

bay haunts and the summer hangouts—the development of the vegetative cover may lag behind. The muskie has no choice then but to drop
down.

However, most fishermen do not follow. Muskie fishing traditionally
is a shallow-water sport, since it primarily involves casting. Trolling
becomes popular later in the season when fishermen correctly realize
that muskies are frequenting deeper water.

Locating muskies in deep water is more difficult, however. In addition, the traditional muskie-catching weaponry—lures and
methods—has evolved without much thought for deep-water angling.
A few muskie fishermen are only now pioneering the use of down-riggers,
perhaps the only practical tool for fishing depths of 25 feet or more.

As a result, most muskie fishermen have poor success in the early
season until the weedbeds have developed and the muskies, in a sense,
come to the shallows where the angler is fishing. This is reflected in a
1975 survey of Muskies, Inc., members who reported the depths at
which 632 muskies were caught:

Depth	Percentage of Muskies Caught
4-feet or less	12%
6-feet	12%
8-feet	18%
10-feet	24%
12-feet	18%
15-feet	12%
20-feet or more	4%

By no means is it a sin to concentrate on shallow-water fishing.
Muskies are in the shallows for varying lengths of time throughout the
angling season. Even in the late summer period, when muskies are
known to prefer the water's deeper structure, there will be movements
into shallower terrain, if only to the top of a sunken island. Under
most conditions these movements take place at dusk and dawn or into
the night.

Shallow-water angling, according to the tastes of muskie fishermen,
plainly is more interesting. In depths of 25 feet or less, the caster and
the troller have some visual mark to relate to. You can pitch to the island shores or methodically troll the points. In that sense, shallow-

water fishing enables the angler to maintain his own bearings. Working deep water often results in a sense of aimless wanderings with the only hope being that you'll stumble into a suspended muskie. It doesn't have to be that way; there are limited methods of selectively scouring possible deep-water haunts.

But as a general rule, the odds of making fish contacts start to decrease in deeper waters—be they walleyes, largemouth bass or crappies.

As I contemplate my own muskie successes, compared with the time of year, there is no pointed message. I have fond memories of days in June and of colorful, wind-chilling outings in September.

Reports from fishermen on the eastern side of the muskies' original range indicate that June is the best month. Veteran Canadian anglers look forward to July. Around the Great Lakes states, the consensus is that mid-June is the time to get serious. Still other regions vote for September through late November. Perhaps the best advice yet is to fish for muskies whenever you have the chance.

It is a plain fact that the quest for a trophy muskie could climax at any time. Because it has. The biggest muskie I've ever hooked, a solid 30-pounder, inhaled a small Rapala that was meant for a smallmouth bass in Lake of the Woods. And that was in mid-June, which is considered early in such a northern setting. Unfortunately, opening day of Ontario's muskie fishing season was still 24 hours away.

A Wisconsin muskie club kept track of 59 muskies taken during one season and found that the biggest fish came in June. Businesses and resorters in northwest Wisconsin tallied the timing and size of 2,022 muskies one year. The average size did not vary much from month to month. But in the final analysis, July and November produced the trophies.

But if there is any one time to select intentionally for the purpose of putting a trophy on the wall, it is the autumn of the year. Starting in September. Again and again, the real "hawgs" are led to the scales in the twilight of the season after hundreds of fair-weather summer anglers have come and gone.

A 1970 survey of muskies caught by members of Muskies, Inc., overwhelmingly indicated that the fall season was the best. Art Lawton's world record was taken in September. Of the 12 known dates of world-record catches, one-third were made in September or October. On Minnesota's Leech Lake more than 42 percent of the muskies over 40 inches in length were caught in September, according to a 1974 survey by Muskies, Inc. And on all lakes surveyed, nearly 37 percent of the big fish fell in the same month.

The evidence leaves little doubt. Something happens after the first frost of fall when the fire-colored leaves begin to tumble from the aspen and maple.

That something is a feeding binge. With the start of cool days and nights, the lake waters begin to turn over; that is, the water begins to mix as the chilled surface layer sinks (cool water is heaviest), to be replaced by warmer water, which in turn is cooled, and so forth.

Two additional factors then enter in: the muskie's optimum feeding temperature of about 68 degrees (F) is reached and the second of two periods of fast growth (early fall) takes place.

In addition, many of the muskie's favorite forage fishes, such as members of the whitefish family, move out of the depths and into the shallows. And the muskie follows. Later still, walleyes will move in closer to shore. The muskie, like most fishermen, won't turn down a meal of walleye, either.

There may be other factors yet unknown that trigger the muskie's autumn eating crusade. But the fisherman need only know that such a phenomenon occurs. Nor is it unique to the muskie. Big-bellied bass also are known for their autumn gorging orgies, particularly timed with the return migration of frogs to the lakes. Walleye fishermen—strong willed and able to withstand those frigid, leaden skies of October—will often find schools of lunker walleyes willing to strike. Weeks earlier those same fish won't even wink at anything with hooks.

But there is yet another reason why September is a favorite: the scenery, the weather, the refreshing fragrance of autumn in the air. No man chases muskies while completely oblivious of his surroundings. Or at least he shouldn't. For the setting also is part of the experience.

The heat of summer is pleasant. But I tire of sweat-stinging eyes and parched lips. I don't need blood-stealing mosquitoes at dusk and biting house flies in August. And the tourist crowds with zoom boaters and thoughtless water-skiers are hardly missed at all.

So give me the fall, when the natural world is winding down but doing it with gusto. When the mallards are restless with the urges of migration; when the redwings flock in noisy unison. Let me view the colorama of frosted leaves and breathe the cool, crisp air. For then muskie fishing is at its best. And if you don't catch one, you really don't care.

If fall is the best muskie season, then what part of the day is tops? A good answer may be: whatever your endurance will permit. I know of no fishermen who stay on the water for 24 hours straight, though some seemingly try. Every muskie angler's physical opportunity and endurance to fish varies, of course.

Very simply, nothing beats spending time on the water if you're after muskies. To repeat, you can't do it with a dry plug. Unfortunately even muskie fishermen have other obligations that cut down on his fishing hours: the job, the home, the family. Don't think for a moment that there haven't been muskie-addict households where the spouse has declared: "It's muskies or me." In a few instances, the choice was muskies—but in defense of a muskie addict's priorities, we'll assume that those marriages were hopeless anyway. Although after hanging around with muskie junkies, it wouldn't surprise me to see one take the fish over the family.

Since the days of Izaak Walton, the hours surrounding sunrise and sunset have been famous as ideal fishing times. And nothing has happened since to change that biological clock. Even today's mechanical genius, the computer, agrees with the findings. A trio of computer experts from Minneapolis once tested the theory, feeding the computer various tidbits of information, such as data from fish movement studies, tide tables and so forth. The wizard machine hummed and purred for a second and then spit out the answer: sunrise and sunset.

But not even computers get the last word when it comes to muskie fishing. A Wisconsin survey concluded that no particular hour of the day was any better than the other numerals on the clock. Following the 1970 fishing season, an analysis of muskie successes by Muskies, Inc., members indicated that the best hours were from 6 A.M. to 11 A.M. and again from 4 P.M. to 9 P.M. Still other studies show that afternoons are better than mornings.

In times of bluebird weather—cloudless skies, bright sun, calm winds—many muskie experts will opt for sunrise and sunset.

My own experience points to midday as the most productive time. After several consecutive trips to Minnesota's Boy Lake chain a few years ago, I was almost able to predict the time of day by the appearance of the first muskie. Invariably, it would appear around noon. Why? I don't know. Nor did I trust my observations. For the following day I'd start fishing again in the morning. And never see a thing until noon. An uneventful morning at least meant there'd be something to look forward to.

No muskie fisherman—if he has the time—is going to sit on shore until a computer or anyone tells him when to go fishing. However, the angler with a budgeted schedule may subscribe to the sunrise-sunset philosophy or he may follow his own intuition. Either choice may be correct.

Many fishermen believe and follow the popular Solunar tables, a listing of predicted major and minor activity periods for fish and wildlife. Those anglers who have had correlated success (that is, their best fishing came at the time the tables predicted) are staunch defenders of the system, which was invented by the late John Alden Knight. The 1974 catches by Muskies, Inc., members showed little correlation to the major and minor Solunar periods. But for every ten fishermen who don't believe, you can find another ten who won't touch the water unless the charts say so.

Several years ago, a computer-drawn timetable of good and bad fishing times was concocted by DataSport, Minneapolis. Again, the inventors fed the computer various bits of research data about nature's biological clocks, tide phases, moon phases, sun positions and selected observations by fishermen, hunters, naturalists and biologists. The computer was able to assemble, compare and otherwise juggle the information in a matter of minutes, whereas the human mind might require years to examine the data from every angle.

The DataSport timetables have been neither conclusive nor inconclusive, although steady users have observed rather consistent correlations. But so far, like the Solunar tables, the computer too has its admirers and detractors.

Despite seasons, hours, tables, Grandma's trick knee or whatever other guidelines fishermen may use to predict their luck, the daily weather often has far more influence. Grandma's trick knee may act up when the relative humidity changes but, so far, there's no evidence that the muskies give a hoot.

For some reason the idea has persisted that ideal muskie fishing weather is hot, humid and calm. Time and again you'll hear a fisherman declare that he ought to be fishing muskies instead of bass because there's not a ripple on the water and the sun is brighter than Liberace's sport coats.

Certainly muskies have been caught in such weather. And surface lures usually aren't effective unless the water's surface is fairly quiet.

The highly publicized Leech Lake, Minnesota, muskie rampage in

1955—when the muskies went nuts and committed suicide on fish hooks by the dozens—was preceded by a couple of weeks of hot, muggy, absolutely windless weather. Similar weather for that length of time has not occurred since. And neither has the rampage.

Nevertheless, the definition of prime muskie fishing weather appears to have been carved in stone following the weird happenings on Leech Lake. And most anglers have read it.

That's fine. But it's not the weather that most of the expert muskie hunters look for.

An overcast day with a slight chop on the water will send learned muskie fishermen scurrying for the boat. And if there's a thunderstorm pending, so much the better.

The same weather formula usually is preferred by walleye and bass fishermen as well.

The overcast and chop cuts down on the amount of sunlight penetrating the waters. And the reduced light apparently triggers increased feeding activity, at least often enough to sell fishermen the idea.

The wave action of course may increase the free oxygen in the water, a factor that also could spur fish activity. In addition, the reduced sunlight and choppy surface make it more difficult for a muskie to see its most persistent enemy: man. In clear waters, muskies are quite capable of spotting a fisherman standing in a boat for distances of 30 feet or more. The muskie depends considerably on its eyesight, not only to find and catch prey, but to survive as well. That is why the muskie is normally associated with clean waters. While muskies still survive in rather muddy rivers within their range, they have disappeared in many silt-laden, polluted, dark-water streams.

The barometer is another favorite choice for predicting fishing success. Generally most anglers, including muskie addicts, like to see a rising barometer. A steady reading or extreme highs and lows are not considered to be ideal fishing times. However, some bass studies, in which fish were observed, have concluded that the barometer has been given unearned importance as a guide to fishing times. The Muskellunge Club of Wisconsin kept weather records from 1968 to 1971, during which 375 muskies were caught. And what was the barometer doing when each of those muskies grabbed the hooks? The barometer was falling during 33 percent of the catches; it was rising for another 36 percent of the fish, and it was steady while the remaining 31 percent of the muskies were hooked. Apparently you can take your choice of favorite barometer readings.

Wind direction and speed is another story, however. It's said that the fish bite the least when the wind is from the east. For as long as I'm able to hold a fishing rod, I'll swear that the scourge of an east wind is the unabashed truth. Yes, I've enjoyed some rare exceptions, particularly after an easterly wind has prevailed for several days. But otherwise the advent of an east wind—and it's usually strong and gusty—has meant the end of fishing and the beginning of misery.

The Wisconsin Muskellunge Club found that an overwhelming majority of their muskie catches, 75 percent, occurred when the wind was southerly. What's more, their luck improved with a southwest wind.

Wind speed also appeared to be important. Some 75 percent of the muskies were caught while a slight ripple or chop covered the water's surface, caused by winds of up to 10 miles per hour. On windless days, 20 percent of the muskies were waylayed. The rest of the muskies, 5 percent, came out of rough seas, winds over 10 miles per hour.

The perfect weather forecast might then read like this: "Mild temperatures with overcast skies and light southwesterly winds; occasional drizzle or showers expected in the afternoon. Possibility of heavy thunderstorms later in the evening."

Often, the more raingear I've had to wear the better the muskie action. Other muskie addicts have had similar experiences. Doc Cotton, who has taken as many as six legal muskies in one day, lives on the shores of Leech Lake near Walker, Minnesota. "When I see it start to rain, I head for the lake," he declares. He doesn't go out to collect soft water in his tackle box or dodge lightning bolts. Muskies just seem to turn on to rain, and I know not why. Again, it may be that the rain reduces the sunlight, thereby encouraging another period of activity.

Ted Capra, another of Minnesota's more distinguished muskie enthusiasts, also is a lover of miserable weather. Some of his biggest muskies have been boated in a downpour. Does a man need more reason?

About the only weather that can discourage even the most diehard muskie fisherman is the appearance of a cold front.

This weather nemesis is so named because its arrival is usually associated with a sudden drop in temperature and strong winds, usually northerly. I use the qualifying word "usually" because meteorologists tell me that cold fronts can occur without any distinct change in the thermometer. But the other identifying characteristics are there: cloudless skies, gusting winds and bright "high" sun.

A cold front with cold conditions is the worst, however. A few years ago Al Lindner, one of the most talented fishermen in the country, kept track of his daily fishing successes as a guide working out of the Nisswa Bait Shop in Minnesota. He had to fish for whatever his customers wanted, of course—walleyes, bass, northern pike, crappies, muskies, you name it. After each outing, Lindner recorded the weather details, the catch, the baits, the depths, the location.

After one season and nearly 200 days of fishing, Lindner found that he had been skunked twice. Both days were cold fronts. On further examination, his "almost skunked days" also were associated with cold fronts.

Quite often the day the cold front arrives is not the worst fishing. That distinction is reserved for the second day. At best you can expect a healthy cold front to knock the hell out of fishing for at least two to three days. Gradually the angling action will improve as the effects of the front—such as a decrease in surface water temperature—are modified.

Ray Ostrom, the Rapala man who knows every muskie hangout in Lake of the Woods, has the best definition of a cold front I've ever heard.

"A cold front is so terrible," says Ostrom, "that for 36 hours afterwards the muskies still are at the bottom of the lake under two feet of mud with their fins over their eyes."

Some muskie fishermen also look (howl?) to the moon for hints of muskie rewards in the offing. But so far research hasn't indicated that there's much connecting muskie fishing and moon phases.

It is interesting to note, however, that every 60-pounder recorded in the *Field and Stream* contests was caught when the moon was dark and nearest the earth.

That means, of course, that Art Lawton's world record, though hooked in late morning, was caught during a dark moon. I'm not sure what that means.

Except Lawton is damned lucky there wasn't a cold front.

Muskie legends are real or imagined. (Photo by Wis. Dept. Natural Resources)

They say it takes 10,000 casts for a muskie. Or does it? (Photo by Jeff Zernov of the In Fisherman)

The muskie strike, sudden and vicious. (Photo by Jeff Zernov of the In Fisherman)

There's room in the jaws of a muskie for almost anything. (Photo by Jeff Zernov of the In Fisherman)

Some tales and dreams come true.

Scenes from Minnesota's Leech Lake in 1955, the summer of the muskie rampage. More than 160 muskies were caught in a two-week period. (Photos by the Grand Rapids *Herald-Review*)

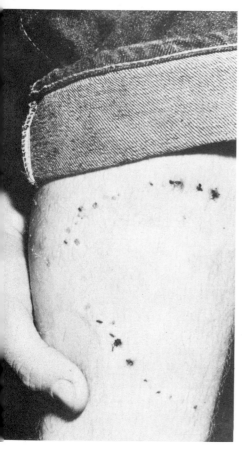

An oddity: the leg of a young water-skiier after being attacked by a muskie on Michigan's Lake St. Clair. (Photos courtesy of Homer LeBlanc)

A leap. (Photo by Jeff Zernov of the In Fisherman)

One muskie caught and one bad case of the fever. (Photo by Jeff Zernov of the In Fisherman)

World-record muskie fisherman Art Lawton holds one of his "smaller" muskies, 65 pounds, 13 ounces.

Lawton's wife Ruth with a 49-pounder.

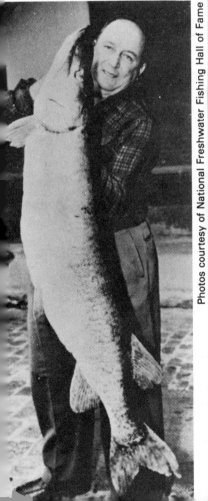

Another famed muskie fisherman, Len Hartman, with a 67-pound, 15-ounce trophy, the fourth largest ever caught on hook and line. (Photo courtesy of National Freshwater Fishing Hall of Fame)

Delores Ott Lapp with her world-record hybrid muskie, 50 pounds, 4 ounces, caught in 1951. (Photo courtesy of National Freshwater Fishing Hall of Fame)

Early-day fishermen with a good old day's catch. (Photo courtesy of Jack Keiser)

Muskies were exploited by both commercial and sport fishermen.

Most commercial netting of muskies ended in the 1930s . . . in time for this lunker to reach 53 pounds, 12 ounces before Myrl McFaul of Wisconsin caught it in 1953. (Photo courtesy of Worth Tackle Co.)

The big question is, can you still find muskies this long? (Photo by the Wis. Dept. Natural Resources)

The future of muskies depends on management and stocking.

Signs like this one are designed to help fishermen learn to distinguish between those two lookalikes, muskie and northern pike.

Under good management, muskies will continue to reach trophy size.

This pair of Minnesota walleye fishermen caught a surprise one day on Leech Lake, a 51-pounder. (Photo courtesy of Walker Chamber of Commerce)

It'll take two fishermen to handle a whopper. (Photo by Jeff Zernov)

Chan Cotton preparing to release a small muskie. (That's not lipstick he's wearing; it's lip salve to protect against sunburn.)

Why fish for muskies? The angler's face tells the answer. (Photo by the Wis. Dept. Natural Resources)

He's not wrestling an alligator, just admiring a muskie.

If you want action, the muskie is the right fish. (Photo by Glenn Lau)

A well-equipped muskie boat. (Photo by Jeff Zernov of the In Fisherman)

A selection of lure types: jerk baits, bucktails, and diving plugs.

The bass boats, made famous by bass fishermen, are ideal muskie-casting platforms.

Popular topwater plugs: Burmek, Cisco Kid Topper, Mud Puppy.

Muskies never have a full complement of teeth. But they always have enough to do the job. (Photo by Glenn Lau)

Popular muskie bucktails, including Mepps, Hildebrandt, Worth, Lindy Spot, Harasser, and Lindy Tandem Spinner Bait.

Other muskie foolers: topwater, jig and eel, spoon, spinner bait, and crank bait.

Mark B. Windels took this 37-pound, 49¾-inch beauty from the Mississippi on August 22, 1975 with a white Harasser.

Illinois muskie angler Larry Ramsell poses with one of the few muskie trophies he hasn't released to fight again.

(Above) Michigan's noted Homer LeBlanc shows why his trolling methods work on Lake St. Clair. *(Below)* Gil Hamm, founder of Muskies, Inc., holds a foot-long muskie ready to be released.

10

Tools of the Trade

A dead worm is but a dead bait, and like to catch nothing, compared to a lively, stirring worm.

—Izaak Walton

Muskie fishermen are the heavyweights of freshwater angling.

The typical muskie rod has the flexibility of a pool cue; a reel is a well-oiled winch. The line would work on a tow truck. Baits can be any size so long as they're big.

In preparation for my first muskie trip, I remember grabbing the stiffest rod I owned. I shook it just to make sure the action wasn't noodle-like. That much I knew about muskie fishing: you go heavily armed.

But I only used that rod once. My first muskie fishing partner, Dick Knapp, handed me a shallow-running Cisco Kid plug. On the first cast I almost sent my scalp flying with the Cisco Kid's treble hooks. The rod was much too light and whippy. Knapp immediately suggested that I borrow one of his spare outfits. His offer was made most graciously—although as I think back, he probably was concerned about his own scalp since we were casting from the same boat.

Muskie fishermen, of course, always are thinking big. Big fish, big rods, big lines, big lures. It only makes sense. Not that muskies haven't been taken on cane poles and handlines. Generally, however, the muskie fisherman heaves weighty lures, ranging from one half ounce to more than three ounces. The mere casting of such heavy hooks will

stress most conventional fishing rods and snap lightweight monofilament lines.

I remember a muskie fishing day with Ted Capra, one of
Minnesota's best muskie fishermen, but also a man willing to try new
gear. He had a new solid, all-plastic rod that was supposed to possess
unusual power and sensitivity. Ted liked the rod's feel and its form-fit-
ted handle. And he used it most of the day, throwing a large Eddy Bait.
He was impressed, since the rod had been designed largely for "heavy"
bass fishing, for pulling crank baits and snaking big bass out of brush.
All went well for several hours when—in one cast—Ted was left
holding the "nice" handle. The rest of the rod was in-flight, like a
spear gone beserk.

It wasn't faulty workmanship that busted that rod. The heavy Eddy
bait had placed such a load on the rod's flexing capabilities that finally,
when it could not bend any more, it broke. Right at the handle.

I, too, have tried at times to get by with light line. Ten-pound test
monofilament in the hands of a skilled fisherman is perfectly capable of
landing any muskie. And there are times when lighter line may per-
form better than the heavy 25- to 30-pound stuff, particularly on certain lure types and weights. But you don't use 10-pound test line with
the heaviest muskie plugs. I once sent a Bobbie Bait through the air on
a record cast for distance. Only my light line no longer was attached.

However, muskie fishing has evolved as a heavy tackle sport for
another important reason: the muskie itself. When a muskie strikes it
will often, an instant before the attack, coil into an "S" shape, then un-
wind at blazing speed to nail its prey broadside. Lures or plugs are
usually smashed in the same manner. That means the lure is broadside in the muskie's mouth, clamped securely within its powerful jaws.

But that also means the hooks may not be buried. More than one
fisherman has assumed that the muskie on the end of his line is hooked.
After all, the fish and the fisherman had been battling. You can imagine the angler's surprise then when the muskie decides merely to
open its mouth and let the plug slip free. The muskie and the fisherman were connected only by the muskie's grip on the lure, nothing
more. When the muskie decided to release its intended meal, the fight
was over.

That's why it's important to set the hooks on a strike. And that can't
be done consistently with a fishing rod with a bullwhip action. With
even the sharpest hooks, it takes power to bury trebles in a muskie's
toothy jaws. And that power must come from the rod.

Trolling fishermen don't have that problem. A muskie usually hooks itself when it collides with the fast-moving plug. Nevertheless most trollers also use heavy outfits because of the strong drag of the line and lure in the water and, of course, the jolting strike.

Not that there isn't room for lighter, more conventional fishing gear in a muskie fisherman's arsenal. Sometimes muskies are looking for snacks, lighter meals. Sometimes they'll ignore large baits and quickly inhale small lures of the size usually thrown at bass or northern pike. No way are you going to throw a quarter-ounce spinner bait with a muskie rod that has the flex of a fence post. And no way are you going to cast a light lure any distance with 30-pound monofilament. The laws of physics just won't permit it.

The angler's choice of rods, reels, lines and so forth are strictly personal. And should be. You'll do best with the gear you're most comfortable with so long as it's adequate for the job. An improper match-up between the rod's action, the line weight and the lure weight will make muskie fishing a miserable experience, except you'll become an expert at diagnosing backlashes. Beyond that, don't exchange an outfit that you can handle simply because it's not the latest model. Too many fishermen make the mistake of being technical gadgeteers. They are equipment freaks, able to describe every detail of the latest reel on the market. But I have yet to meet one who could fish worth a damn. A good fisherman will surround himself with proper gear that's in working order and let somebody else worry about the technicalities of fiberglass rods.

Now for a closer look at:

Rods: Every muskie fisherman should own at least two, if not three fishing rods. (No, I don't work for a rod builder.) The reason is simply that no single rod design will fulfill every fishing situation, particularly for casting. The angler who trolls almost exclusively doesn't have that problem. Usually one rod will suffice for anything he wants to pull through the water, short of an anchor. But even the serious troller may carry a spare rod in the event of a breakdown.

(Of course this discussion has no bearing on the number of rods an angler may legally use, according to the fishing laws in each state or province.)

The trolling fisherman need worry only about choosing a rod that can withstand the drag of the line and lure and still have reserve flex for the strike. Hefty canepoles will even do the job.

The fisherman who likes to cast has to be more selective, for he acts more intimately with his gear. And his performance will depend much on the selection of his mechanical fishing partner. Most casters carry two rods of different designs, one to handle the heavy jerk baits and deep-running plugs, the other to cast the lighter bucktails, tandem spinners or shallow-running plugs.

And when the fishing starts, both rods will be outfitted and "at ready," complete with attached lure. No, you can't cast with a rod in each hand, although many muskie addicts wish they could. There's a very practical reason for having two rods ready for action. Many times a muskie on the follow will look at the lure only once and forget it. Other times you may get a swirl past a lure as a muskie charges up to take the hooks but changes its mind at the last second. When that happens, a quick-thinking angler will drop one rod and pick up the other, which, of course, has a different-type lure. Immediately, he'll throw the new bait to where the muskie was last seen. Many times, the new lure or color will then entice a serious strike.

I remember once seeing a muskie "roll" around a magnum Rapala I was retrieving. I recast the Rapala and again the muskie gave it a look. I switched rods. This time I threw a black Suick, gave it two jerks and . . . kaboom. The muskie had the Suick. Or at least I think it was the same fish. But I'll never know. That particular muskie threw the hooks at boatside.

The typical muskie-designed fishing rod on the market is stout from the butt to the tip. It is designed that way to handle the lures, not the fish. While the muskie is a good fighter, it isn't capable of splintering fiberglass. Yet a novice, upon seeing such a stick, will think it is necessary to subdue those colossal muskies he's heard about. Not so. But the novice need not be disappointed. The stoutness still is an aid in setting the hooks in those colossal fish.

The specially designed muskie rods will range in price from $20 to $150, with most in the $20 and $40 category. In your selection, at least, stick with a well-known brand name, such as Heddon, St. Croix, Fenwick, Lindy-Little Joe, Browning. The rods generally run from five and one half to six feet with straight or offset handles. Some salt-water popping rods also have the same desired action. However, the handles on various saltwater rods may be long and cumbersome to a muskie fisherman, unless used for trolling.

The new graphite rods, recently introduced to the market, have much potential as a muskie stick. The graphite rod is light and powerful with much faster setting power than the popular fiberglass models. So far, most of the graphite makers have concentrated their efforts on flyrods and conventional spinning or bait-casting models. However, muskie-designed graphites are finally showing up on the market.

I have used a special six-foot, six-inch muskie graphite, custom-designed by Burger Bros. Sporting Goods, a large Minneapolis tackle outlet. The rod is a piece of art. Casts are made effortlessly with the graphite's quick loading power for lures ranging from one half ounce to two ounces. And its lightness is well appreciated after hours of fishing.

Graphites are considerably more expensive than fiberglass rods, although as rod builders improve their technology and more rod makers enter the market, the price should go down. Of course there are cheaper graphite imitations already on the store counters. If you're looking for the advantages of graphite, make sure the rod is made of 90- to 100-percent graphite. The imitations are mostly fiberglass with a token use of graphite—just so the word "graphite" can be used in the advertising pitch.

If you're still wondering what all the excitement is about over graphite, go test cast the rod. Don't just hold it or shake it. Cast it. You'll be amazed. The graphite may not be the final answer in rod materials but it's earned a place on the rod rack.

The second fishing rod found in most muskie boats is considerably lighter than the stout sticks used for trolling or heaving giant plugs. The second rod is characterized by having a more flexible tip, tapered to a fairly stout butt. Such a rod is best for casting the lighter muskie lures up to about one-ounce weights, such as the bucktails, tandem spinner baits, shallow-running plugs or even the miniature jerk baits. Its use as a trolling rod would be secondary.

Manufacturers usually list these muskie rods as "heavy bait casting" or "lunker sticks" or "bass worming rods." Don't worry about the name. Just examine the rod maker's suggested lure weights; if the rod will handle up to one-ounce lures, you're probably in the ball park. Again, stick with the brand names, such as those mentioned earlier.

Reels: The three basic reel styles—bait-casting, open-face spinning and closed-face spin-cast—will all work for muskie fishing. But by far the most popular in muskie fishing circles is the bait-casting, free-spool reel, equipped with a star drag. As usual there are reasons for it. The bait-casting reel is a hardy model, built for long, strenuous casting chores. In addition the star drag system is undoubtedly the best. And a good-working drag is important for setting the hook and playing the fish. Most good free-spool reels also may be adjusted to the weight of the lure being used, thereby reducing backlash problems. Of course, everybody gets a backlash now and then on a bait-casting reel. (When it happens to me I call it a "professional over-run.")

Another advantage of the bait-cast reels is the high-speed gear ratios being offered for fast retrieves. A troller could hardly care less about gear ratios or retrieves, of course. But to the caster, such detail is important. For a high gear ratio means fewer turns on the reel handle in a day. In addition, if you want to retrieve a lure rapidly, it can be done for hours with the right gear ratio without suffering muscle cramps. A ratio of 4:1 or 5:1 is preferred. A bait-cast reel with large handle grips is another desirable feature. The line capacity of a reel is not usually something to worry about. Most models easily handle from 100 to 200 yards, depending on the diameter of the line. A muskie reel should have a minimum of 100 yards of line to cover the length of your casts and the feet of line lost in clipping frayed ends. Most conscientious muskie addicts will automatically discard several feet of line nearest the plug after several hours of service or after a muskie has been hooked. This is done as a safeguard to avoid the possibility of unknowingly using frayed line.

You'll have fewer reel headaches by choosing brand-name bait-casting reels, such as Garcia, Penn, Quick, Heddon, Shakespeare, Diawa.

The open-face spinning reels, usually the heavy-duty or saltwater models, also are very adequate. By all means if you feel more comfortable with a spinning versus a bait-casting reel, go ahead and use it. Your only disadvantage is in the drag system, which is not as smooth and sophisticated. However, the casting may be more trouble-free. You need not worry about thumb pressure and backlashes, although I've suffered some terrible "bird nests" and jumbled line on spinning reels as well. With spinning reels, just remember you'll be using fairly heavy line so you'll need adequate spool capacity. Among the popular brand names are: Zebco Cardinal, Quick, Penn, Garcia, Diawa, Heddon, Shakespeare.

Spin-cast or closed-face reels are the least popular among muskie fishermen, although such reels may be the easiest to cast. However, most spin-cast models are designed for the fishing masses, the vacationing angler. Few of the spin-casts are built to withstand the extensive casting abuse that the muskie fisherman is capable of delivering. Nevertheless the spin-casts will work. And if you're in the market, choose the more robust models that are built for heavier lines. Two manufacturers that offer such models are Zebco and Johnson.

Lines: The two basic lines in popular use for muskie fishing are monofilament and braided Dacron. As for a recommendation, it's a tossup. Every fisherman has his own theories. But there are a couple of points to keep in mind. The braided line is thicker; that is, its diameter is considerably greater than monofilament except in the larger weights. And in some cases—in extremely clear waters—the visual differences between mono and braided may make the difference in the number of muskie strikes. Fishermen who troll often prefer lines of the smallest diameter possible of adequate pound test. The "thinner" the line, the less resistance in the water and the deeper a lure may travel. Speed trollers also like line, such as No-Bo, with very little stretch because they depend on the collision—between lure and fish—to set the hook. A line with excessive stretch may lessen the impact of that collision, resulting in a poor set.

The knot strengths of various lines is also an important consideration. While monofilament brands may appear to be very similar, they may have considerable differences in knot strength. An easy test is to take a short strand of monofilament and tie a simple overhand knot in the center. Then pull from each end, slowly, until the knot breaks. The line that requires the most "pull" before the knot breaks is the line with the best knot strength.

The braided lines generally are considered to be the toughest. Unlike monofilament, braided line will not cut itself And usually Dacron will survive intact if a hooked muskie wraps the line around weed stems or rolls the line around its body as muskies tend to do.

Whatever line is chosen, it should be of adequate pound-test.

Experienced muskie anglers generally use line weights of 25 to 40 pounds. Probably the absolute minimum to be considered is 15-pound test. Again, you may want to use several different line weights to fit a particular situation. For example, the lightest line should be used when fishing with a jig or jig-eel combination to obtain the best jig action.

But under most conditions, the stouter lines are preferred. Most muskie lures are large enough so that the stiffer, heavier lines will not interfere with a lure's action. Equally important, lines of 25- to 40-pound test offer peace of mind and room for error. Simply, it takes more fraying, more nicks and more antics by a muskie before such lines develop a breakable weakness.

Knots: There are more ways to entwine fishing line than any fisherman needs (or wants) to know. And I shall not bore you with a discussion about my own knot inventions . . . most of which break under pressure anyway. But what fisherman hasn't played with inventing knots? They are so damnably important. Whole books have been written exclusively about knots. But this book isn't one of them.

My old flying instructor once told me that any landing I walked away from was a good one. So too with knots. Any knot that holds is a good one. It doesn't even need an name.

Personally, knot-tying has not been my specialty. If I piloted a Cessna the way I tie knots, I would have crashed and burned a long time ago.

However, through some sympathetic friends I've come to learn enough knots that hold to fit almost any fishing situation.

These are the Spider Hitch, Surgeon's Loop, Blood, Palomar and the Improved Clinch. (To tie, see diagrams.)

And a word about each.

The *Spider Hitch* is a poor man's Bimini Twist knot, easier to tie but just as functional. The Spider Hitch creates a double line with 90 to 100 percent of the strength of an unknotted line, making it ideal for muskie fishermen who don't like steel or braided wire leaders. The knot is further unique in that, if one of the two lines should break, the other will still hold. The lure or a swivel-snap is tied direct to the terminal end of the loop.

The *Surgeon's Loop* also makes a double line loop, although it is generally used when a smaller loop is desired.

The *Blood Knot* is used for connecting two ends of monofilament such as a shock leader. While it looks complicated, it is not particularly difficult to tie or remember.

The *Palomar* is an excellent 98- to 100-percent knot for connecting a lure or a swivel snap directly to the line. Note the advantage of a double line.

The *Improved Clinch Knot* is probably the most popular knot for tying anything to anything in the fishing world. The Improved Clinch also is a 98- to 100-percent knot, although it must be tied correctly or the entwined monofilament will cut itself. Make sure that the line is wrapped evenly for a minimum of five turns before the knot is snugged tight.

One of the newest knots to come along is called the "Uni-Knot," which is practically a system all its own. The basic Uni-Knot was invented by Vic Dunaway of Florida. According to tests by the DuPont Company, the Uni-Knot holds from 95 to 100 percent of the line breaking strength. Since the knot has several possible uses for muskie fishermen, the Uni-Knot system works as follows (courtesy of DuPont Company):

In learning the system, you must first master the basic Uni-Knot, as used to tie line to the eye of a hook, swivel or lure. Here are the steps:

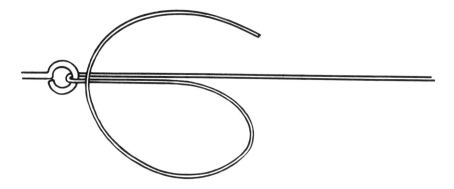

Run the line through the eye for at least six inches. Fold it back to form a double line and make a circle back toward the hook or lure with the tag end.

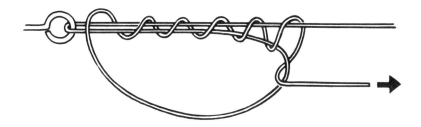

Make six turns with the tag end around the double line and through the circle. Holding the double line at the point where it passes through the eye, pull the tag end, as indicated by arrow, until the six turns are snugged into a tight barrel.

Now grasp the standing part of the line and pull (see arrow) to slide the knot up against the eye.

Continue to pull standing line until knot is tight. You can trim the tag end flush with closest coil of the knot, because the Uni-Knot doesn't allow line slippage.

To tie a small loop to the eye of a lure, giving it free movement in the water, tie the same knot, up to the point where the turns are snugged up around the standing line.

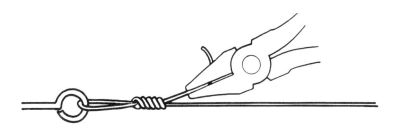

Next, slide the knot toward the eye of the lure by pulling on the standing line until the size of loop desired is reached. Use tacklebox pliers to hold the knot at this point, pulling the tag end to maximum tightness.

Under normal casting and retrieving the loop will hold. Once a fish is hooked, the knot will slide tight against the eye for better security.

In joining two lines of about the same diameter, overlap the ends of the lines, about six inches. With one of the ends form the Uni-Knot circle, crossing the two lines at about half the overlapped distance.

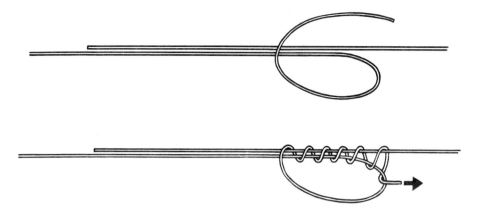

Make six turns around the two lines and through the circle, as in the basic knot. Pull tag end in direction indicated by arrow to snug knot up tight around the other line.

This will leave the other half of the overlap unknotted. Using loose end of overlapped line, tie another Uni-Knot and snug up.

Now pull the two standing lines in opposite directions, as shown by arrows, to slide the knots together.

Pull as tight as possible and snip off ends close to nearest coil.

Leaders: To a muskie fisherman, the leader is the business end of his fishing gear. You can have the best lure in the world but if the business end doesn't hold you might as well cast or troll a lunch bucket . . . you end up with the same results.

Leaders may consist of several different materials: single-strand wire, braided wire, plastic-coated wire, heavy monofilament or nothing.

Some muskie fishermen don't believe in or use anything for a leader except the regular line on the reel and a swivel or snap at the end. They are willing to take their chances, believing that they'll get more strikes without a heavy leader (reducing visibility). In addition, some lures (such as the Rapalas) have sensitive actions, which are hindered or completely eliminated by the weight and stiffness of a leader.

Nevertheless, a leader still makes sense. Only a few muskie lakes, particularly in Canada, are so clear as to force an angler to go to lighter line and no leader. In those instances where a leader may interfere with the action of a lure, simply test the lure's action by the boat first. If the leader makes a difference, go without one until you switch to a plug that isn't affected.

The whole idea of a leader is to neutralize the line-cutting teeth of a muskie. Researchers at Berkley, an Iowa tackle manufacturer specializing in lines and leaders, once tested 20-pound monofilament in the mouth of a captive 35-pound muskellunge. After a few chomps of the muskie's jaws the line samples were examined. The breaking strength of the line had dropped by more than 30 percent, and the line's toughness (its resistance to rupture) had decreased by 60 percent.

Let there be no doubt, the muskie is well equipped to snip most monofilament sizes without missing a stroke. While a muskie usually strikes from the side or from the rear, occasionally the fish will attack from a forward position, sweeping its gaping jaws toward the head of the lure. Without a leader the ball game is usually over when that happens. What's more, you've lost the lure as well.

At other times, a muskie may inhale a lure so deeply that the line also is clamped within its jaws.

A hooked muskie is notorious for "rolling" and "somersaulting." Unless you're lucky, you'll find the muskie suddenly has rolled itself up on the line. When that happens, you're in trouble. The muskie's gill covers are sharp and also quite capable of neatly cutting most monofilament. But not even steel leaders are much help in this situation, since the typical leader used is from nine to 18 inches in length. One roll of a good-sized muskie will use up that much. Trollers will often use 30- or 36-inch leaders for that reason. But such lengths are impractical when casting.

As a further defense against the muskie's teeth or its rolling tactic, the use of a "shock leader" is often employed. A shock leader is simply a series of different line strengths tied together with the heaviest pound-test nearest the lure or leader. For example, if the reel is filled with 25-pound test line, some fishermen will tie—using a Blood Knot—a 10-foot section of 30- or 40-pound test monofilament at the terminal end. The knot should be trimmed so that it passes easily through the rod guides. In addition, coat the knot with Pliobond, a liquid rubber-based cement. When dried, the Pliobond forms a smooth "bulge" over the knot, allowing easy passage through the guides while protecting the knot.

As for metal leaders, the choice of style and length is rather irrelevant. Plastic-coated braided wire is popular because of its strength and flexibility. It is larger in diameter than uncoated or single-strand wire leaders, however. The braided wire comes in various pound-tests, no different from braided or monofilament fishing lines. Leaders of 25- to 40-pound test are most popular.

The plastic-coated leaders offer another advantage in that no knots are required. Simply form a loop, then twist the tag end about four times around the standing part of the leader and apply heat, such as a match. The melted plastic will fuse and make an extremely strong connection after it has cooled. You'll want to place a lure or swivel in the loop before the heat is applied to the twist, of course. The method is quick and simple, enabling you to make your own leaders on the spot to meet any situation.

Among the commercially made leaders, some of the better-known brands are: Seven Strand, Weller, Sampo and Berkley.

Swivels and snaps also deserve attention, since they also are at the business end of the line. A weak snap can lose a fish and a bad swivel can twist the line or kink the leader, thereby weakening both.

Snaps come in two basic styles—the safety pin design and the hook design where the snap-wire hooks on a post. Both snaps will do the job. The important step is to choose a snap that is strong enough for the job. Snaps and swivels, like lines, also are rated by pound-strengths.

Unless size is important, most muskie fishermen select snaps and swivels rated up to 100 pounds.

The ball-bearing-designed swivels are the most trouble-free. To test a swivel, to make sure it twists freely, tie a piece of line to each end of the swivel and apply pressure, pulling from each end of the lines. Then rotate one of the lines. The swivel should turn freely. If it doesn't, you're asking for problems.

In summary, there is no single absolute, proper, faultless method of securing the terminal end of your fishing line. There are successful muskie fishermen who set forth with every possible combination—from no leader at all to six-foot lengths of single, double or braided steel line and 100-pound snaps and swivels. And every combination has a use.

The lesson, however, is to pay considerable attention to the business end of your line. Don't use materials that impede a lure. On the other hand, don't seek that muskie trophy with a terminal end that is needlessly vulnerable. You owe that much to yourself and the muskie, because if it's hooked you'll stand a fair chance of landing the fish unless it spits the hooks. To send a muskie back to the water with a mouthful of barbs—thanks to a faulty snap, a bad leader, a poor knot, or a frayed line—isn't anybody's idea of happiness, your's or the muskie's.

Lures: Let's make one thing perfectly clear. Man has inhabited this earth for something like two million years now, and he's been sport fishing for several hundred. Yet in all that time, the only invention that comes close to guaranteeing fish is the gill net. And it's illegal in the name of hook and line fishing.

This point is made to protect the innocent. Namely myself. A discussion of lures preys on emotions. It's the fisherman's version of opening Pandora's box. And I'm not about to choose sides.

There is no best lure. If there were, there would be only one on the tackle shelves. There is no best color, shape, price, name, or weight. If you're looking for secrets, there are none. If it's made in Hong Kong, so what? What in hell do they know about muskies?

The only way to size up lures is to examine what muskie fishermen use. And they use everything from hand-painted bat handles to frogs and suckers.

As one muskie nut put it, "Anything works so long as it's large, has plenty of action and moves fast."

The size of a lure or bait is one of the muskie fisherman's least concerns. There simply isn't a plug on the market that is too big for a muskie to handle. A muskie is willing and able to swallow a meal half its own size. That means a "small" 30-inch muskie could indeed take a 15-inch sucker, for example. Of course, there are times when small lures are more effective. But generally muskie fishermen subscribe to the theory: Big Bait, Big Fish.

The shape means nothing either. One time Keith Gardner, editor of *Fishing World* magazine, visited Minnesota for a muskie fishing trip and tied on an Alou Cowkiller plastic eel. Gardner's Swedish guide was flabbergasted, "My God, lookit dot big vurm of yours." Gardner didn't nail a muskie with the contraption. But then you'll note that the guide was unwilling to predict its failure.

In a 1974 survey of Muskies, Inc., members, some 30 different lure brands were named as having taken at least one muskie. That's what I mean about Pandora's box. The right lure at the right time is the one that works.

Of course muskie fishermen have their favorites which, through the seasons, have proven effective. These fish foolers are generally divided into the categories of: bucktail spinners, jerk baits, diving plugs, topwater plugs, spoons, and live bait.

By far the most popular of these lure types is the bucktail spinners. And in comparison studies, the bucktail comes out as the most effective lure. However, that conclusion, too, must be tempered by the fact that the bucktail spends more time in the water than most of the other lure designs. For example, many muskie fishermen believe—and some studies show—that the jerk baits (those that are jerked or twitched through the water) tend to attract larger muskies.

A breakdown of the lure types and their effectiveness in catching muskies looks like this:

Muskies Caught Per Lure Type*

Lure Type	Percentage of Muskies
Bucktail Spinners	47.0%
Jerk Baits	16.0%
Top Water	2.0%
Diving Plugs	20.0%
Spoons	1.0%
Live Bait	7.0%
Others (jigs, etc.)	7.0%

*Compiled from data furnished by Muskies, Inc., and the Vilas County (Wis.) Muskie Marathon contest.

The low rating for live bait may be rather surprising. A live sucker—the real thing—is of course the most perfectly designed "lure." Every tackle maker in the country tries to imitate the real thing. But a great majority of muskie fishermen prefer to use artificials, probably because there's more of a challenge and sense of satisfaction. A Wisconsin survey showed that some 85 percent of all muskie fishermen used man-made baits exclusively.

In addition, the muskie fishermen who intend to release every muskie not measuring up to trophy size prefer artificials for the ease of releasing the fish. A muskie that has swallowed a sucker may be too severely injured to release with much hope for survival.

In other comparisons, live bait does significantly better. In a Wisconsin survey of 465 muskies caught, 173 were taken with live bait, 157 with bucktails, 71 on diving plugs, 33 on spoons, 11 on top water and 20 on miscellaneous lures.

Do some lure types tend to haul in larger muskies than other lures? Sometimes. After 12 seasons in Wisconsin's Vilas County muskie contest, the jerk baits had accounted for seven of the 12 largest fish. In another Wisconsin contest, the Bobbie Bait—one of the popular jerk baits—took the largest muskie in three out of five years. During the 1975 Wisconsin season, a study of 369 muskies, taken from 88 lakes, showed that 345 were taken on artificials, 24 on live bait. The most effective lure was the bucktail, but the jerk baits captured the largest muskie.

However, in the 1973 Muskies, Inc., members contest, there were 93 muskies caught over 38 inches in length. Of the big fish, 61 were fooled by bucktails, 18 by jerk baits, 12 by diving plugs, one by top water and one by live bait.

The smaller muskies (179), those under 38 inches, were caught thusly: bucktails, 44.7 percent; diving plugs, 30.7 percent; jerk baits, 18.4 percent; top water, 3.9 percent; and live bait, 2.3 percent.

In this example, the overall most popular lure, the bucktail, was the trophy-producer with the jerk bait second. It is interesting to note, however, that the jerk bait—typically the largest plug used by muskie fishermen—did not appeal to muskies under 38 inches in length.

Perhaps the big plug, big fish theory is more fact than fiction.

Not all muskie fishermen are content with the lures they find on the store shelves, of course. So they make their own. My friend Tom McNally, outdoor writer of the Chicago *Tribune*, once told me about using a piece of rope to take northern pike. So I made a rope lure for muskies. Never have caught anything with it. But it's been worth a few jokes. Apparently northern pike are more gullible for rope.

But other do-it-yourselfers have had better luck, though not a whole lot. In 1974, lures made by Muskies, Inc., members took eight of 283 muskies. While that's nothing to shout about, the anglers who made those baits and then actually caught a muskie are undoubtedly on Cloud Nine yet.

Most muskie addicts are content to select their secret weapons out of the tackle shops and catalogs, however. The following is a list of the more common brand names for each category of muskie lure: BUCK-TAIL: Mepps, Worth, Hildebrandt, Lindy-Little Joe, Marathon, Grassl's, Mr. Twister, Harasser, Hawg Spin. JERK BAITS: Eddy Bait, Bobbie Bait, Teddy Bait, Suick, Rapala (optional). TOP WATER: Jitterbug, Globe, Cisco Topper, LeBoeuf Creeper, Mud Puppy, Injured Minnow. DIVING PLUGS: Cisco Kid, Creek Chub, Rapala, Rebel, Bomber, Musky Ike, Burmek, Whopper Stopper, Cordell, Bagley, Heddon. SPOONS: Daredevle, Johnson, Lindy-Little Joe, Nebco, Doctor, Red-Eye, Buck's.

By no means is the list complete. There are simply dozens of manufacturers of spoons, spinner baits, bass crank baits, jigs and so forth—and all are potential muskie lures. The names listed, however, appear most frequently in a muskie fisherman's tackle box.

Aside from choosing a lure, there's the important task of keeping the hooks sharp. Suffice it to say, it takes very little time to touch up a dull hook with a sharpening stone and to bury 3/0 and 5/0 treble hooks you'll need all the help you can get.

It's also good practice to occasionally check the screws and hooks on a lure. Screws have a way of working loose and hooks can get bent. Again, such maintenance chores take so little effort but mean so much.

About the time you ignore such items, you'll suffer the common muskie fisherman's plague: You'll lose the biggest muskie you've ever had on.

Nets, Gaffs and Clubs: These are the tools of the happily nerve-wracked muskie fisherman. For when you reach for the net, you may be one step from scooping up a dream come true. Obviously this is no time to blow it.

The most important consideration in choosing a net is strength, particularly where the net handle and the hoop join. Make sure that intersection is reinforced. More than one muskie has been lost when the net handle snapped at that juncture. A good muskie net also should be deep, 48 to 60 inches, and the hoop should be at least 30 to 36 inches wide so there's plenty of room to steer a muskie into the net headfirst without catching the hooks.

Gaffs are often preferred by fishermen who become skilled in using one, although most muskie anglers feel more comfortable with a net. In choosing a gaff, however, make sure the hook is of a heavy gauge wire.

Most gaffed fish are hooked from below, either in through the gill cover opening or up through the lower jaw. Still other anglers prefer to gaff the fish from inside the mouth down through the lower jaw behind the jawbone.

If you plan to keep the muskie, use a club, such as a hammer or small baseball bat. By all means, dispatch the muskie before it is heaved into the boat. To be in a boat with a wild, frantic muskie with a mouthful of treble hooks can be very dangerous. Or, at the very least the muskie will upset every tackle box in the boat before it can be subdued. A solid, sharp blow at the base of the skull should do the job.

Years ago, muskie fishermen carried pistols to waylay their muskies. The method worked, although it was highly dangerous and was finally outlawed. The muskie was shot while lying in the water and then was lifted onboard. You had to be cool and calm, however. If you forgot the order in which the job was done, well . . . your boat would sink. Don't think it didn't happen.

Tackle Boxes: Muskie fishermen are not renowned big spenders on tackle boxes. The usual plug carrier is nothing more than a lidless styrofoam cooler with the lures stuck around the top. Woven picnic baskets also are common. There are commercial tackle boxes, however, specially designed for muskie plugs. And there are plug carriers that can be hung along the gunwales of the boat. No matter how the plugs are transported, the element of safety should be considered. Lures may be the playthings of older boys but they are not toys.

Boats and Motors: Frankly, if you're crazy enough to fish for muskies you can fish out of anything that floats. Very little effective muskie fishing is done from shore, except in rivers where fishermen may wade and fish from pool to pool.

The choice of boats and power is also a matter of personal taste. Except there are some points to consider. If you basically prefer to cast for muskies, you might consider a boat with plenty of open, level deck space on which to stand. Unless you always fish alone there should be room fore and aft so that two fishermen may cast without whistling lures by each other's ears. The fanciest casting platforms on the water these days are the so-called bass boats, such as the Ranger. Despite the name, they make excellent muskie boats as well. Other conventional aluminum fishing boats have been modified to suit the muskie angler, such as Lund's Pike boat.

The troller does not have to be concerned about casting room. A good trolling boat has comfortable seats, however, complete with rod holders. Beyond that, there are no particular requirements in a trolling rig.

The proper casting or trolling craft should be suitable for the waters to be fished for safety's sake. If you consistently fish big waters, such as Michigan's Lake St. Clair, you have no business buying a 12-foot dinghy. On the other hand, if your choice of waters is the St. Croix River, the dinghy will be more than adequate. Common sense should be the judge.

A muskie could care less about what's pushing your boat, an outboard, inboard-outboard or inboard. The choice is immaterial.

Most trolling is done at five to 10 knots. Hence, many trolling boats will have big horsepower for traveling and a smaller "kicker"—five to 15 h.p. for trolling. While the large outboards can idle down to the proper trolling speed, such slow idling for long periods of time tends to cause fouling problems. Those 100 horsepower jobs weren't designed for poke-along speeds.

The casting muskie fisherman often likes to drift and cast, so the power requirements also are not critical. When there's no wind, the electric trolling motors are ideal, clean and quiet. For a variety of speeds and power, the 12- to 24-volt electrics work best, running off of one or two marine batteries connected in a series. Most electrics are available with manual or foot controls. The choice is yours.

11

Muskie Methods That Work

T'was the day of the season and all through the lake
Not a muskie was striking, not even a snake.
I tossed out a Rapala—new green for the year.
A lure not even giants would look at and fear.

When all of a sudden, there rose a huge splash,
A 30-pound muskie hit like a flash.
I tightened the hook and my knees had a jiggle,
The huge fish dove—right out to the middle.

My stomach rolled over, I shouted with glee.
My eyes were all frosted, t'was impossible to see.
But do not conclude 'cause my line then went soft,
God Bless America, the son-of-a-bitch got off.

—by the author

There are many, many simple methods for catching the mighty muskellunge.

It's important to keep telling yourself that. Particularly when you haven't had a strike in a week. Every muskie fisherman from Day One has thought, at one time or another, that he'd found the secret formula, the never-fail recipe for putting a muskie in the boat. And every one of those formulas was 100 percent until it came time to try again.

The only technique that pays good dividends is called hard work. The angler who keeps pitching and trying; the angler who uses his mind as well as his brawn; the angler who maintains unswerving confidence in whatever method he uses is the angler who finds no mystery in the muskie.

There is no halfway. Those freak catches are just that. The serious student of muskie fishing is looking for consistency. Muskies by accident are unpredictable. They can happen at any time—to the kid on the dock, the tourist who had never fished before.

But there is no shortcut to consistency. Not that it takes years to achieve. Many newcomers to muskie fishing discover that the muskellunge is not difficult to find if you fish the right waters and it's not impossible to catch if you offer the right baits.

Yet non-muskie fishermen are fond of asking, "How can you do it, how can you continue to fish for muskies?" The question implies that the muskie addict is always fishing for nothing. The noted fisherman-author Jason Lucas once concluded that there were two sure-fire ways for a man to make a fool of himself. "One is to fall in love with the wrong woman. The other is to fish for muskellunge."

Lucas is correct, of course. What does the love song say . . . "Fools rush in . . ." And as a muskie fisherman I have wondered aloud, "What in hell am I doing out here?"

But I knew the answer. And the newcomers and veterans who've done their homework know the answer. By fishing good waters, by practicing sensible methods, by angling with confidence, the pursuit of the muskellunge clearly is one of the most exciting experiences in all of hook-and-line angling. The majority of the nation's fishermen only dream of seeing or hooking 15- to 30-pound fish. The muskie fisherman has that chance every time out. Most fishermen can't imagine what it's like to have mammoth fish swimming inches behind your hidden hooks. Muskie fishermen know: It'll make your knees tremble like an aspen leaf. Your heart will lodge in your throat. And you'll t-t-t-talk l-l-l-like . . . th-th-th-this. If the giant swims away, normal speech will return in the form of four-letter words. If you land that trophy, you'll t-t-t-talk l-l-l-like t-t-t-this for a mo-mo-mo . . . week.

Any muskie method will provide such unabashed intoxication. You can cast live muskrats and half-grown ducks and take a muskie. (The fish has been known to devour such critters, but it's difficult to find a bait shop that stocks live muskrats. There are artificial lures that are patterned after such things as ducks, muskrats, or mice, however.)

The muskie's eating habits, and the productive lure shapes and colors, bear little resemblance to each other.

Most of the original muskellunge waters are marked by having good populations of whitefish, ciscoes and suckers. These soft-finned fish provide excellent forage for muskies. However, the muskie doesn't appear to be choosy about what it likes to eat. Except it must be alive first. While some studies have indicated the muskie goes for soft-finned fish over prey with spiny-rayed fins, a Canada study showed that yellow perch (with spiny-rayed fins) made up 55 to 70 percent of the muskie's diet.

Obviously what the muskie eats depends on what's available. Larry Porter, a zealous student of muskies and a Muskies, Inc., member, compiled the results of three different muskie food reports, totaling 80 fish. The stomach contents showed that perch was the most frequent food, followed by suckers.

The breakdown looked like this:

Stomach Contents	Frequency
Perch	41%
Suckers	18%
Bass, sunfish	14%
Bullheads, catfish	9%
Walleyes	8%
Whitefish, ciscoes	7%
Northern pike, muskie	2%
Mooneye shad	1%

(Not included in the food breakdown was a leopard frog taken by a 35-inch muskie and a fully grown muskrat inhaled by a 53-incher.)

Porter also computed the average length of the food found in the muskie stomachs. Then he compared the food length with the length of the muskie itself.

The comparison supported what most muskie fishermen have long believed: The larger muskies consume the larger meals.

Here are the results:

Comparison of Muskie Length and Food Length*

Muskie Length	Average Length of Food
30 inches	3.1 inches
31	4.0

Muskie Length	Average Length of Food
32	4.8
33	5.7
34	6.6
35	7.5
36	8.3
37	9.2
38	10.1
39	10.9
40	11.8
41	12.7
42	13.5
43	14.4
44	15.3
45	16.1
46	17.0
47	17.9
48	18.7
49	19.6
50	20.5

*compiled by Larry Porter, member Muskies, Inc.

Porter further expanded the length of muskie/length food relationship and estimated that a 55-inch muskie could be expected to eat prey nearly 25 inches long. A 60-inch muskie might grab another fish almost 30 inches long. Art Lawton's world-record fish, 64 ½ inches long, easily could have swallowed a 34-inch meal. In fact, when Lawton finally brought the world record to the boat he said the huge fish regurgitated an estimated 2-pound northern pike.

The contents of a muskie's stomach may, of course, be misleading since the smaller prey digests more quickly. Many muskies also expel part of their food while fighting the hooks.

Nevertheless Porter's table shows that you can troll the largest muskrat you can find and still expect a strike.

Since you really can't use too big a lure, there aren't many excuses left . . . unless the muskie has a sore mouth. Now there's a time-honored excuse the muskie and northern pike fishermen use to the hilt: "Can't catch 'em because they've lost their teeth and their gums are sore."

An early-day muskie fisherman once wrote: "About the middle of August the muskie loses his teeth and his mouth is in such shape that it takes something mightily aggravating to arouse enough anger to make him forget his sore molars and strike."

It's a beautiful theory, a natural cop-out for a luckless muskie trip.

Unfortunately the sore-mouth story is also an old wives' tale. Perhaps it's time to bury this colorful but false bit of muskie lore.

The teeth involved in the sore-gum theory are the knifelike canines that line each side of the lower jaw like a rack of spears. However, the meat-eating muskie leads a life of violence. And most of that violence takes place within its jaws. As a result, the canines are constantly being broken, injured or otherwise lost. But they are constantly being renewed, too. The muskie can ill afford to compete for survival armed with smooth gums.

In an examination of some 200 northern pike and muskies, none had a full complement of teeth. Most barely had three fourths of their teeth. Muskies have between 14 and 18 canine teeth per jaw. But only about six to 11 are ever in service at one time.

Undoubtedly some fisherman long ago discovered that some teeth were missing and invented the sore-mouth theory. Little did he know there always are teeth missing.

Scientists have examined the loose teeth in muskies and the apparent inflammation of the gums. They have concluded that the looseness is a normal condition of some teeth and the redness simply is the result of normal blood flow to the gums. The redness also increases when a tooth is being replaced; however, there is no proof of soreness.

Of course the muskie jaws that fishermen examine belong to fish that have been caught. The fact that the muskie had been fighting with a mouthful of hooks could be a reason for reddish or bleeding gums.

When muskies are tougher than normal to catch, it usually means the fisherman is not fishing where the muskie is or he's competing for the muskie's attention with an abundant food supply. Captive muskies in aquariums have been known to fast for several weeks at a time. But again there was no evidence that the muskie's lack of appetite had anything to do with dental problems.

Now that the handy excuses have been stripped away, it's time to be practical. Forget the baloney. Build your confidence on the foundation that there are fishing methods that take muskies rather consistently.

And if they don't work today, there's always tomorrow. The plastic worm is acclaimed as the best artificial bass fooler ever devised by man. But the worm doesn't fill the boat with bass every day. Nor do you melt the worms down into a plastic ball when they fail. Same with muskie methods. Don't abandon time-proven techniques. By all means experiment, but devise those experiments from the lessons of what has worked. For example, expert muskie fishermen have long known that small quarter-ounce bass-sized spinner baits and the alphabet or bass crank baits are particularly effective on muskies during the early-season period. As the summer progressed they'd then switch to the larger, more conventional muskie lures.

But somebody finally said, "Hey, if those smaller lures will take muskies in the spring, why not later?"

Sure enough, the experiment—a slight modification from a known method—has worked surprisingly well, particularly on stocked muskie lakes with a rather high population of 30- to 36-inch fish.

Minnesota's Ron Lindner, publisher of the In Fisherman angling course, also toyed with known bass fishing techniques with muskies in mind. He looked at the conventional quarter- to half-ounce spinner bait, those safety-pin-styled lures with blades and skirts of wild colors. Lindner thought, "Why not take a good lure and make it bigger?" He did, and the muskie tandem, a jumbo-sized spinner bait, was a reality. And some of those wild colors, like bright orange and black, worked as well.

Consider the old idea about muskies being strictly loners. That is, if you caught one at Point A you had better move to Point B. There's mounting evidence that shows that could be the wrong decision.

I have raised positively three different muskies within a 10-yard patch of vegetation without moving the boat. Al Lindner once counted 25 muskies all moving in unison across a shallow bar. Many other muskie fishermen have at one time or another raised or caught more than one muskie from the same spot. Wisconsin fisheries biologist Leon Johnson reported electro-shocking schools of muskies. Johnson also noted that muskies are not necessarily stay-at-homes, that they tend to move from one haunt to the next, possibly as the food supply shifts. There was one particular muskie, however, that was found in the same spot for eight years!

If you see a muskie in one area and fail to catch it, it still makes sense to return to the spot later. A muskie probably will be there. It may not be the same one but . . . at that point, who cares? And if you nail one muskie, you don't necessarily have to roar across the lake to help your partner find a fish. Muskies appear to have some gregarious tendencies and may actually hunt or travel in schools of two or more. The point is they are not always loners.

While casting and trolling are the two basic methods of muskie fishing, each method involves other important choices: the hours, the depths, the lures, the color and so forth.

In the 1975 Muskies, Inc., members' contest, various data were kept on the 632 muskies caught during the season. The information was fed into a computer by Denny Gebhard and Don Lomax, the inventors of DataSport, an annual booklet of computer-drawn charts showing the best and poorest fishing hours each day.

After analyzing how 632 muskies were caught, the computer provided the following information:

Best Lures: Mepps Giant Killer Bucktail and Cisco Kid
Best Single Color: Black, Yellow, Green
Best Color Combination: Green-yellow
Best Depth: 10 to 12 feet (but near 20- to 35-foot depths)
Best Cover: Weedbeds
Best Hours: 11 A.M. to 11:30 A.M. and 3 P.M. to 4:30 P.M.

The computer's hour selections may be more indicative of fishermen's habits than best fishing times, however. As the computer analyzed the data, very few muskies were caught between noon and 1 P.M. That could mean that's a poor fishing hour. Or it could mean that's when most fishermen take a lunch break. In addition, few muskies were caught between midnight and 5:30 A.M. Probably because normal muskie anglers are sleeping then.

Keep in mind that a computer has never caught a muskie. Yet the color choices indicate what most muskie fishermen prefer. And the color combination of green-yellow closely mimics the colors of perch, a muskie's favorite morsel.

A Look at Casting versus Trolling

Trolling is generally considered to be the most effective method of muskie fishing. While the casting fisherman may fish likely muskie haunts more thoroughly, the troller covers more haunts in less time. Since the muskie is a low-density fish, (meaning few individuals per acre of water) it behooves the angler to cover as much water as possible. For that reason, it perhaps is no coincidence that most of the world records were taken by trolling.

Some state natural resource departments, such as Wisconsin, have prohibited or restricted trolling because of its effectiveness.

Yet despite its track record, trolling is disliked by many muskie fishermen. It is boring. Compared to casting, trolling is like watching grass grow. Among the casting die-hards, it is considered to be a lazy, amateurish method, largely a meat operation.

But perhaps the primary objection is not what trolling is or does but what it doesn't do. Trollers seldom if ever see a muskie follow. While you can't weigh a follow or hang it on the wall, a muskie close behind a lure, within arm's length of the boat, is one of the most exciting moments in angling. And most casting fishermen wouldn't miss it for the world, even if it means long hours of heaving and retrieving a plug. Of course the serious troller thinks casting is a tedious assignment. And on goes the debate. Which is rather funny. Because non-muskie fishermen have the opinion that muskie fishing, trolling or casting, is nothing but a big drag.

The smart muskie fisherman will practice both methods. Even the most athletic fisherman will suffer tired arms and casting cramps. And his confidence and concentration will wane.

The troller, too, will get the same symptons, losing confidence and not concentrating on his speed or direction. That's the time to change. Switching tactics is a great morale booster—even for just a short period of time. And it's quite necessary. The search for a muskie taxes both a man's patience and stamina. You will have times when your efforts seem futile. And the hopelessness of it all will gnaw relentlessly, weakening your will to go on. But you will continue. Because you want a muskie. So you'll troll some more or cast some more. It's the only game in town.

Casting Methods

The casting muskie fisherman must have several talents. He must master his equipment; he must properly work a lure and he must control his boat.

Since every cast counts, you are only penalizing yourself when every other cast results in a backlash. If you're trying a new reel, take a few practice casts in the backyard before you head to the lake. Carry reel oil in your tackle box. If you're serious about casting, you'll need it.

Watch your backcast. A good way to lose a fishing partner is to whip a pair of treble hooks past his nose. Make sure you're comfortable with your rod and reel. Some fishermen wear gloves on one hand or the other to prevent blisters and sore spots. Carry extra reel parts, such as the nut on the reel handle. The damned things always come off.

While the troller fishes entire shorelines or reefs or what have you, the caster fishes spots. Thus boat control is tremendously important. It does no good to select a likely-looking "spot," then have your boat drift out of casting range. Or worse, right on top of where you wanted to cast.

The caster's best friend is a gentle breeze or wind from the proper direction. For by drifting with the wind you can approach your fishing spot quietly and pass quietly, except for the splash of a falling lure. As you drift, cast downwind or perpendicular so as to cover the water before the boat does.

If you're drifting along a weedbed, work the outside, or deep-water edge, first. Then move back up and drift the inside edge. If near shore, don't ignore the piers and docks, particularly those nearest the weed-line. Docks and piers attract small fishes and provide overhead cover—two of the muskie's favorite luxuries.

In strong winds, casting and boat control become very difficult, of course. Since you'll drift too fast to cast ahead of the boat, cast sideways or perpendicular to the wind. Or fish the more sheltered shores.

Backtrolling is another method of combating strong winds. By running the outboard in reverse, you can slow your drift as the backward thrust of the prop acts like a brake. Or you can start downwind and backtroll slowly against the wind, casting as you go.

Various studies have concluded that engine noise, except in shallow water (less than 10 feet), has little effect on fish if the engine noise is steady.

But never roar up to your chosen fishing spot, cut the engine and expect to pull out a trophy. Most veteran muskie anglers are convinced that such a tactic alerts the wise muskies. Whenever possible, approach a muskie hangout as quietly as possible, using the wind to bring your boat silently within casting range. When you think about it, what have you got to lose? Fish may not be bothered by the sounds of an engine prop, but there's no doubt the noise is heard. Trollers of course always have an outboard or inboard-outboard running and the lures often are trolled near the boat. Indeed, the muskie doesn't seem to be frightened. But it may be adding apples and oranges to conclude that a caster can do the same. The troller is constantly on the move, whereas the caster is more stationary. While those differences may seem slight the caster has the choice of being noisy or quiet. It only makes common sense to choose the latter.

The casting muskie fisherman has another advantage with lures. He has a wider assortment available and he's in a position to work any lure more effectively. Unlike a troller, the casting angler may not be able to use a deep-running plug all day, simply because retrieving such lures is exhausting. But otherwise, the caster is free to put his imagination and ingenuity to work.

Casting the Bucktail

Bucktail spinners are by far the casting angler's favorite. Most are easy to cast, easy to retrieve. And the bucktail provides most of its own tantalizing action, meaning almost anybody can fish it properly.

Because of the bucktail's advantages, it undoubtedly sees more action than any other lure style. And, as a result, most studies show that the bucktail has caught the most muskies. The most popular colors are: black, yellow, white, purple, red, brown or natural. While black appears to be the most consistent muskie producer, a muskie fisherman should equip himself with a variety of colors. As usual, there are days when black is useless.

There's an old adage: dark days, dark colors; bright days, bright colors. It's an adage worth remembering . . . at least for a starting point. On those bright calm days in clear water, many muskie fishermen will go to the red bucktail. For no reason except that it's proven successful under those conditions in the past.

If the action is slow for any color bucktail, the addition of a white pork rind or twister-type plastic tail on the trailing hook may attract a strike. A strip of plastic or rind (one to four inches in lengtn) can be added to almost any lure to make it more enticing. But make sure that is the result. Sometimes even the added weight or drag of the pork rind will destroy the action of certain lures. In the event a single trailer hook must be added to the lure, face the trailer hook downwards. It will be more effective in that position, unless you're fishing in weeds. Then, the trailer hook should face upwards to make it as weedless as possible.

While the bucktail spinner doesn't need much help, fishermen often make three common mistakes. They fish the bucktail too slow, they fish it in deep water and they don't use it often enough. Chan "Doc" Cotton, an avid and successful bucktail fan, cranks the bucktail about as fast as a high-speed reel will go. Doc's theory is that the bucktail's speed may discourage follows but it appears to encourage strikes.

For all of the bucktail's magic it is not a good deep-water lure, simply because it sinks too slowly (wasting time) and it doesn't stay deep. Nor was the bucktail designed as a diver. It is best when used alongside weedbeds or over the top of submerged vegetation. Despite its adequate supply of hooks, the deer-hair tail tends to act like a weed guard. While the bucktail isn't totally weedless, it will slice unmarred through an amazing amount of vegetation.

When retrieving the bucktail, it is possible to give it a jerky, erratic action. Such variety definitely is worth trying. But generally a straight, fast retrieve is best.

I usually give the bucktail a sharp twitch at the start of the retrieve to start the spinner blades turning. Then, at the end of the retrieve—before the lure reaches the boat—I'll swing my fishing rod to the right or left to make the lure abruptly change directions. Often a muskie that was content to simply follow the straight-running lure will be enticed to strike as the lure darts to the right or left.

Of all the common muskie lures, the bucktail has the reputation for being the surest-hooking lure. Since it is lighter than most jerk baits or diving plugs, there is less danger of the bucktail flying loose when a muskie goes airborne. In addition, the treble hooks on bucktails usually are smaller, affording deeper penetration than the aforementioned plugs.

One comment about the blades on a bucktail. The blades come in various sizes and colors. Undoubtedly the most popular size is the No. 5 blade. Colors range from nickel to brass to copper to painted blades of any color. Again, on dark days start out with the brass or copper blades; bright days, nickel or white. But I can't say I've ever really noticed a difference in blade colors as compared to bucktail colors. The choice is available anyway.

Most importantly, there should be a bucktail or two in every muskie fisherman's repertoire. Even trollers. For the bucktail is an effective trolling lure. To be without such a reputable muskie catcher is like having an outboard with no prop.

The large muskie-sized spinnerbaits or muskie tandems are similar in nature to the bucktails. However, the tandem (two-bladed) buck-tails tend to pull with more resistance through the water. The spin-nerbaits have one advantage in that the tandem blade will "flutter" as it sinks. That advantage is best put to use over weedbeds where you might allow the spinnerbait to drop into weed pockets and flutter downward. Bass often hit such a tactic. So will muskies.

The tandem spinnerbait also runs slightly deeper than the conven-tional straight-shafted bucktails. But it is most effective in waters of 15 feet or less.

Unlike the bucktail spinner, the tandem spinnerbait is seemingly more effective fished slow with its large blades pulsating sensuously. That's fortunate. It's impractical to retrieve the large tandems with any quickness because your cranking hand will go numb first.

Like the bucktail, there is no better time to use the spinnerbait.

Anytime is good for both lures.

Casting the Jerk Baits

The jerk bait is the muskie fisherman's idea of heavy artillery. If you've never thrown a jerk bait, tie a cement block to your necktie and flip your head. You'll get the idea. Jerk baits are the big boys, the three-ounce plugs, six to eight inches long with three sets of treble hooks and room for an outboard motor. Casting a jerk bait is no prob-lem. Once you swing all that weight in motion, it flies forever. And forever. I once handed a jerk bait to Wally Hilgenberg, a muscular linebacker for the Minnesota Vikings football team. I said, "Cast it." I don't think the plug has hit the water yet.

Jerk baits are the muskie fisherman's symbol. It's the largest plug made for freshwater fishing. Only the big lake trout spoons come close, but they're gentle looking compared to the hook-infested jerk baits.

But it's also a plug that is useless without a good fisherman at the other end. For most of the jerk bait's action is what the fisherman gives it—a series of soft, short, steady . . . well, jerks. Let your arms and the rod do the work. You may want to sweep the rod to the right, come back and quickly take up the slack, then sweep to the left, come back, take up the slack and repeat. This imparts a zig-zag action to the jerk bait as it slowly dives and rises, dives and rises like a sickly sucker. And that's what it's supposed to imitate. A fish near death, too weak to swim downward to the safety of the vegetation and too exhausted to escape. The scenario is enough to make even a muskie smile. And plenty of muskies fall for it.

Jerk baits are tried and true muskie takers. They are not as popular as the bucktails, largely because fishing is supposed to be fun, not punishing. And throwing jerk baits for any length of time is defined as hard labor. Nevertheless, jerk baits are known as the trophy hunters. They will attract the larger muskies. But setting the hook is not always easy. The lure is heavy and it's usually clamped crossways between a muskie's jaws. Once the strike is detected (it's often visible), it's best to set the hook hard at least three times. Your best hope is that the muskie, upon sensing the false meal, will release its grip on the jerk bait at the moment you are trying to set the hooks.

Jerk baits come in a variety of colors with black again the most popular color. Other successful color combinations include perch, walleye, off-white or black-white. Your choice of colors may not be as important as your choice of the lure itself.

It's important that the lure be well balanced. The Eddy and Teddy baits, for example, should only barely float with the head end pointed slightly downward. The Suick and Bobbie baits should float evenly, the depth being controlled by bending the metal tail. Without a properly balanced jerk bait you'll be hard pressed to give it a tantalizing action.

A jerk bait pulled straight through the water has virtually no action. As such, it is seldom used by trolling fishermen.

Casting the Diving Plugs

Diving plugs are the work horses in a muskie fisherman's tackle box. They are made in dozens of styles and colors. Some sink, some float. Some bump the bottom; others weave, wiggle, jiggle, wobble or otherwise look like they're alive and very eatable.

They are very popular among muskie fishermen for the same important reason: they're effective and easy to use. Most models are neither difficult to cast nor physically tiring to retrieve, except for the very deep running models.

Again there is little the fisherman has to do with the lure except pull it through the water. All of the diving plugs have built-in actions by the various lure makers.

However, of all the lure types, the muskie tends to follow the diving plugs most frequently. Not that that's a criticism. Follows are better than nothing. But you can often turn that follow into a strike by "ripping" or "lifting" hard on the diving plug as it nears the boat. Again this abrupt change of direction in the lure may excite a muskie into striking.

Of course, the diving plug is the trolling anglers' bread and butter lure. By simply choosing a shallow, medium or deep-running plug, the troller can cover water depths from about five feet to 20 feet without adding weight.

Casting fishermen use diving plugs for the same purposes, of course. Along deepwater weedline drops, along points, over sunken islands and so forth.

The diving plugs generally are not good weedbed lures, however. Most are anything but weedless and, in fact, are capable of severely damaging good muskie habitat.

While the early diving plugs generally had long, slender shapes—à la natural bait—the fishing world has seen the advent of the fat-bellied, pregnant plugs of bass fishing fame. Muskie fishermen are discovering them, too. While the chubby plugs, called crank baits or alphabet lures, are not the size of conventional muskie diving baits, they have a future in muskie fishing circles.

Casting the Topwaters

Surface strikes make memories. A man can catch a lot of fish in a lifetime of angling, but he'll remember best those sudden, violent eruptions around a topwater plug.

Although bass have the reputation for smashing things on the surface, a muskie has no qualms about it either. In fact a muskellunge hits the top with a flair for the dramatic. My most vivid memory is of a 12- to 15-pound silvery muskie on Rainy Lake—a muskie I never hooked. It was an absolutely still day. I was swishing a mud puppy across the mirror surface only inches above a thick weedbed. Suddenly the water parted not 15 yards from the boat. The muskie shot above the surface like a shiny missile. For a moment it was as though everything was frozen: the water flying; the wild-eyed muskie suspended in midair. And I shall not forget the sight, the excitement. At the time I was disappointed about missing the strike. For some reason that matters no more.

Topwater fishing for muskies is not practiced by most muskie fishermen. Granted, it is not the most effective technique. It can be the most exciting, however. Topwater fishing requires certain conditions, usually a calm, windless day when the gurgling or sputtering sounds of the surface plug can attract a muskie's attention. Evenings or early mornings—when the winds have died—are the prime times.

Topwater plugs also are particularly effective over dense weedbeds that lie just under the surface. Aside from a weedless spoon, no other lure can be thrown into the "cabbage" with much effectiveness.

Even the topwater lures will occasionally become entangled in the floating leaves or stems, though they are weedless for the most part.

There is no proper way to fish a topwater. Some fishermen prefer to retrieve the gurgling plugs at a slow, steady pace. Others will "buzz" the topwater rapidly or make it skitter, stop, skitter, stop. Still another technique is to fish the topwater much like a popping plug. Twitch, rest, twitch rest and so forth.

On the strike you should delay a count or two before setting the hook. Sometimes the hook will already be buried in a muskie's jaws, simply by the force of the strike. If the muskie misses, let the plug sit motionless for a few seconds. Then give it a short twitch. And look out. If the muskie was serious, it will often attack again.

The color of a topwater probably isn't too important. Black, frog-colored or red-white are popular.

But every muskie fisherman ought to toss a topwater now and then. Or twitch a floating model diving plug, such as the Rapala, on the surface. One strike will make a memory.

Casting the Spoons

Spoons undoubedly are used by more fishermen to catch more different species of fish than any other lure. When you think of northern pike lures, what comes to mind? Only the famed red and white spoon. Yet few fishermen throw spoons for the muskellunge, a close relative of the northern pike. Why? I'm not sure. Except that spoons don't appear to be as effective. That's probably reason enough. However, most muskie fishermen I know carry a spoon or two, regardless. Like the diving plugs or bucktails, the spoon provides its own action. It's easy to cast and not tiring to retrieve. And it is another lure that works equally well in shallow or deep, for both trolling and casting. The weedless spoons, of course, are ideal for working dense weedbeds or flooded timber, the most famous being the Johnson Silver Minnow and pork rind combination.

No doubt the most popular colors for muskies are the good old red-white, followed by black-white and red-yellow.

The fish-catching ability of spoons is hardly debatable. It's a universal lure. If I could fish around the world but with only one lure, it would be a spoon. Yet the muskie, of all fish, doesn't seem impressed.

Casting Jigs and Things

The lead-headed jigs—a gob of lead molded around the eye of a hook—are only lately becoming more popular in the muskie fishing fraternity. Black, white and green jigs—from a quarter ounce to an ounce—have become favorites, particularly during early- and late-season muskie fishing. Usually the jig is adorned with a large live minnow or a plastic eel-like tail and is bounced rather rapidly over the bottom or over deep-water weedbeds. However, the jig is most often used for muskies in deep-water situations, 15 to 30 feet, to reach down to sunken islands, humps, bars that are often missed by conventional lures.

I know of at least one muskie that was taken on a jig in 80 feet of water. While no one knows how much time muskies spend at such depths, for sure the only quick way to reach fish that deep is with a jig. Many fishermen naturally believe that the majority of trophy muskies are swimming in depths that seldom see a lure. I remember seeing a sounder graph of a deep hole in Minnesota'a West Battle Lake, a lake with a good muskie population. The paper graph, taken by Ken Rustad, showed a number of huge fish scattered at 50-foot depths. Rustad dropped a jig down to the fish but with no luck. Were they huge carp? Nobody knows. But the electronic graph sounder wasn't lying. They were fish, they were big and they were lying at depths where trollers or casters seldom tread.

That's why the jig—as a muskie catcher—may be the lure of the future.

Casting or Trolling Live Baits

Nature's most perfect muskie lure is the black sucker, a prolific, soft-finned fish that occurs naturally throughout most of the muskie's range. Hatchery-raised muskies usually are fed a steady diet of suckers. Native muskies learn early to follow suckers in the spring, for example. You might say muskies are conditioned to take suckers.

While live bait fishing is not the most popular form among muskie anglers, no one argues the effectiveness of the real thing. Most well-stocked bait shops handle muskie-sized suckers, eight to 12 inches long, usually purchased individually rather than "by the dozen."

The sucker can be fished alive or dead. When fished alive, the sucker is usually "still-fished"; that is, the sucker is hooked gently through the mouth or behind the dorsal fin and allowed to swim freely underneath a large bobber at depths of four to 15 feet.

Still fishing then settles into a watch-the-bobber game. When the bobber disappears the game starts to get exciting. The most common mistake made when the excitement begins is setting the hook too soon. Even a muskie takes time in devouring such a meal. Some bait fishermen will wait 30 to 45 minutes before setting the hook. While that much time usually isn't necessary, the longer you wait the better your chances of hooking the muskie. When the time is right, take up the slack in the fishing line and set the hook hard. At least twice. Remember, you're pulling against the sucker as well as the muskie. That's why it's best to use large 6/0 to 8/0 single hooks.

In casting or trolling a sucker, dead or alive, the bait is either hooked through the lips or eyes or rigged in some type of hook harness. A sucker improperly hooked will roll or spin. At best the sucker should swim straight or weave from side to side while remaining in a normal upright position. There are commercially made sucker harnesses, although the homemade varieties work as well (see illustration). A trailer hook, single or treble, tied to the front hook and left free to trail near the sucker's tail, may sometimes mean the difference between success and failure. A muskie that hits the trailer hook will of course be hooked immediately, eliminating the waiting period. But more importantly, the muskie will not be hooked deeply in the stomach. The biggest disadvantage in using live bait is the increased chances of fatally injuring a muskie that you'd rather release. Once the stomach is ripped by a hook the muskie's chances of recovery may be reduced severely.

Trolling fishermen must weight the sucker to keep it down, of course. Lead weights can be jammed into the fish itself; or you can place sinkers on a line approximately four to six feet ahead of the sucker. Because the sucker normally is swallowed, by all means use a steel leader at the terminal end of the fishing line.

Basics of Trolling

Almost any muskie lure, except topwater and jerk baits, can successfully be trolled. Bucktails, while normally considered a tool of the casting fisherman, are in fact excellent trolling lures. But by far the most popular trolling lures are the diving plugs, spoons and suckers.

While trolling looks simple enough—sit back while you pull something through the water—the technique involves more precision.

Speed perhaps is the most important criterion. And most trollers move too slow. Actually it's almost impossible to troll too fast. A muskie is quite capable of short bursts of speed of 30 miles per hour. Many boats can't exceed that rate. The trolling speed is limited by the type of lure used, of course. Most lures are designed for and function best at speeds ranging from three to six miles per hour. You can go faster with spoons, however, and certain specially designed trolling lures, such as spoon plugs.

Generally the faster you can go and still maintain lure control, the more productive your trolling will be. Michigan's Homer LeBlanc, probably the best-known muskie troller, believes speed is the ultimate key to enticing a muskie to strike. With a fast-moving lure, the muskie must either hit or forget it. Whereas a slowly trolled plug gives the muskie more time to contemplate the potential prey, increasing the odds that the muskie may think better of the situation.

One primary advantage of trolling is its effectiveness in deep water. Equipped with wire or lead-core line or by using heavy lead weights ahead of the lure, a troller easily can reach 20 to 40 feet of water, where the trophies supposedly hang out.

The troller's nemesis, however, is weeds. Most weedlines and points don't run in convenient straight lines. And no matter how hard you try to follow the edge of a weedline drop-off or weedbed, invariably you'll hit a small point of weeds and the lure immediately will be out of order. This problem can be reduced by running a shorter line, say 30 instead of 80 feet. With less line trailing behind your boat, you'll have better control of the lure's path.

Don't worry about the prop wash. LeBlanc made a living catching muskies with his self-designed Swim Whizz lure within four feet of the boat and only two feet deep. In fact LeBlanc has had muskies strike the prop like it was just something else to eat. He also believes in speeds of four to five miles per hour.

Some lures won't run at the higher speeds unless adjusted properly.

If the lure runs to the left, take a pliers and bend the eyelet (where the line is tied) to the right. On lures with metal lips, sometimes the lips too must be fine-tuned in the same manner.

Undoubtedly the latest innovation for muskie trolling is the use of downriggers—5- to 10-pound lead weights, which are lowered on a cable to the desired depths. With downriggers you can maintain a fairly steady depth and still use light tackle, since the line to the lure is held to the ball with a snap that releases upon the strike.

Downriggers have been used with good success on Michigan's Lake St. Clair and on several lakes in Minnesota. Of course there's no good reason why the technique shouldn't work. After all, it's merely a variation of straight trolling, except the depth selection is more precise. The question still to be answered is: Are downriggers an advantage that's worth the time and cost?

Muskies in Darkness

Night fishing for muskies is one of the great unknowns, mostly because very little night fishing is done. While muskie fishermen are known to go to extremes to nab a trophy, most still insist on being able to see by sunlight.

Yet it happens. Some venturesome muskie addict will break the rules and be rewarded. But of all the nighttime fishing stories I've heard, Steve Statland's tale of the midnight muskies is the best:

"After a hard day's work and a six-hour drive, the three of us [he and two fishing partners] were pretty tired. Unpacking and rigging tackle took more time, and a good night's sleep seemed in order as it was nearing midnight. But something kept tugging at me. Was it the rays of that big full moon filtering through our cabin window? Or was it something else deeper inside me? I had no takers and a couple of laughs when I asked if anyone would like to join me for a few casts. 'Muskies don't feed at night,' was the comment I heard as I stepped out into the crisp chilled night. Years of experience and many trophy muskies allowed me a silent chuckle of my own.

"The boat glided away from shore as I quietly pulled on the oars. Moonbeams seemed to grab hold of the boat and guide it down a lighted path to a point in the narrows where the boat came to a motionless stop. Arm and rod became one in an effortless toss as my silver Rebel cut through the darkness.

"Probing the depths, the lure occasionally reflected a glint of moonlight as it wriggled through the water. Suddenly the lure wriggled no more as it was jolted to a halt by the viselike clamp of the vicious jaws which surrounded it. The huge fish instantly sailed out of the water trying to repel the sharp barbed hooks which stung in its mouth. But I retaliated with three or four solid jerks on the rod and at that moment the great fish and I both knew we were in for a long battle. She surged powerfully, running off many precious feet of line as the drag hummed. The rod kept the pressure on the fish and when her head was turned she shook violently and then broke the surface of the water over and over again. While I could still not see the fish, her power and weight sent tremors up my arm and her repeated airborne attempts at escape sent shock waves across the surface of the quiet lake. The unrelenting pressure of the seven-foot rod and 20-pound line slowly took its toll and sapped her great strength. She was finally along-side the boat and the landing net dipped into the water to claim its prize. But it came up empty as the muskie made a final desperate lunge for freedom. But the battle-experienced rod was prepared for this maneuver and it dipped sharply into the water and then powerfully raised the fish up and into the net. The muskie was immediately hefted into the boat and the moonlight could only give a clue as to its size.

"My heart pounded, my hands were now allowed to shake, and my piercing victory yell resounded over the lake and echoed through the woods as I gazed upon the great fish. She tipped the scales at 22 pounds, and while I have caught far larger ones, none have held the magic for me as did this one, which charged my bait at midnight under the intoxication of the full moon."

Statland's experience is indeed a true story. But it probably won't convert many anglers into being nocturnal. Most fishermen have other things on their minds at night.

However, Wisconsin's Art Moraski is different. Moraski has spent hundreds of hours of fishing—all in darkness. And when he wasn't fishing he was probing the nighttime shores with search lights exploring and researching the nocturnal movements of fish. While he hasn't fished exclusively for muskies, he has caught muskies at various ungodly hours. And he's had enough success with walleyes and muskies to write two booklets about "Night Fishing" and start a fishing research team in Franklin, Wisconsin.

Moraski is, of course, convinced that muskies feed more at night than most anglers think. Except for the hybrid muskie. In six years of research Moraski has never seen a hybrid (muskie-northern pike cross) feeding in the shallows at night.

However, true muskies may be active at night under any conditions—full moon, dark moon—and are quite capable of seeing or sensing a lure. Moraski once took a muskie in pitch darkness while speed-reeling a Rapala as fast as possible. He's also used bucktails and topwater plugs with good success at night.

While I have had limited experience night fishing, most of it has been bad. The simple act of tying a knot turns into a major undertaking.

But no doubt there's a whole new muskie fishing world waiting to be explored under starlight. The next time insomnia strikes, you might see if a muskie will do the same.

Muskies and Rivers

History indicates the muskie originally was a fish of rivers. Yet today muskies are usually associated with lakes or flowages (dammed rivers). The pollution and destruction of many rivers has eliminated the muskie, of course. Nevertheless the muskie still is an important river fish throughout its range. And quite catchable in such flowing waters.

River fishing for muskies offers several advantages: the moving water usually is more dingy, thereby reducing the problem of bright sun. Rivers can be "read" more easily than lakes, giving the angler an idea of where muskies might be lurking. There's less temperature fluctuation and more uniform distribution of oxygen, thereby eliminating factors that might affect muskies in a lake. As a result, muskies tend to roam closer to the surface in a river. After all, how can they go deep in a shallow river?

However, the typical haunts of a river muskie include the deepest holes, the back eddies, the brush-infested shores and, of course, weedbeds. Unlike the smallmouth bass you'll seldom find muskies in fast water or rapids.

River trolling usually is done with the current. For two reasons. It is difficult to keep a lure down by running against the power of the current. In addition, the muskie is accustomed to seeing its food being carried downstream.

The cast also should be directed across the current or quartered upstream for the same reasons.

Beyond those considerations, any muskie lure that works in a lake will produce equally well in a river.

The Invaluable Figure Eight

The figure eight is the muskie fisherman's last resort. You've made the cast and completed the retrieve, the lure is approaching the boat. You have one last chance to nail a muskie. That consists of sweeping the lure in a figure eight pattern or circle before lifting the lure out of the water.

May I say quite strongly, any muskie fisherman who ignores putting the frosting on the cake—the figure eight—will be sorry sooner or later. Before I learned my lesson a muskie had to nearly jump into the boat as I carelessly hoisted the lure from beyond its reach.

Many muskie fishermen will keep the lure in the water in a circle or figure eight when they see a muskie following. But it's best to add that touch after every cast. Sometimes you won't see the muskie following. Sometimes the muskie will rush out from under the boat. Sometimes it just comes from nowhere.

As long as the lure continues to move, a muskie will stay interested. Stop the lure and you're done. Some fishermen have managed to keep a muskie watching and following for minutes at a time. And as long as it's interested there's a chance for a strike. Even if the muskie doesn't strike, the experience is damned exciting.

The figure eight is most effective if it is made as deep as possible. Don't be afraid to stick the rod completely into the water, up to the reel if necessary.

Admittedly it's difficult to hook a muskie on such short line. However, if your plug and the muskie are still connected after the initial uproar, quickly release the reel brake to give line or reduce the drag.

At that point you haven't won the battle but then you haven't lost it, either.

A muskie fisherman learns not to hope for more.

12

Big Enough to Keep?

When it's all said and done, when a muskie-fishing man has explored all the figures, when he's studied all the lures and memorized all the hot tips, it is time to reflect.

I have labored on this book for more than six months—researching, writing. My mind is jumbled with muskie this, muskie that. It is indeed a time to reflect.

No sermon have I prepared. No philosophical ramblings. No memorable lines of wisdom. No, none of that. Just tell it like it is.

The muskellunge has contributed greatly to the sport of angling. It is a fish of color and lore, of mystery and magnificence. Without the muskie, the family of sport fishes—as great as it is—would be the less. And there'd be a vacuum amid those angling days. But that need not be. Or even feared. It is the angler's turn for charity.

But what can we give that the muskie must have? Clean water is hardly a man-made product.

My friends, you can give only what you decide not to take. To the muskie you can give it its life.

We may think the release of a muskie is a noble gesture. And it is. But to let a "legal" muskie loose to fight again another day is also an admirable act of selfishness. Because the future of trophy muskie fishing is dependent on that release. If the muskie fisherman doesn't do it, who will? If the muskie fisherman doesn't release the sub-trophy muskies to continue to grow—and it will as long as it lives—where will tomorrow's trophies come from?

The solution is that simple. But the problem is very real. The continent's muskies are being "cropped down" by all kinds of pressures. Of which not the least is fishing. We're keeping 15-pounders now when we wish they were 30-pounders. It's like the man who blows his money and then wonders why he's always broke.

Allow me to be selfish for a moment. There is no muskie trophy on my wall. I wish there were. But my 30-plus pounder is still swimming somewhere. And when I see the 8- and 10- and 15-pounders hauled to the docks—muskies far short of being trophy material—I have to wonder. Was that my 30-pounder that was cropped? If that 10-pounder had been released, instead of being hung unceremoniously on a stringer, would it have come back a few years hence as somebody's catch of a lifetime? Would that somebody have been me?

Of course every fisherman "has the right" to keep a legal-sized muskie. And if you've been fishing hard for years or months or weeks or even days, who can fault keeping a 15-pounder if it's your very first muskie. But if your second muskie weighs 14 pounds should it be flopped in the boat, too?

No. If you want to improve your own chances of taking bigger muskies you can help yourself by sending that 14-pounder back into the water.

Is the problem that bad? Are the lunkers that rare? Take a look at the trophy success of a few muskie clubs. Club members undoubtedly represent the cream of muskie fishermen. If anybody could be expected to catch the giant muskellunge, the odds are with a club member who has worked hard to improve his angling skills.

But let's take a look at some 700 muskies caught by members of Muskies, Inc., the Wisconsin Muskellunge Club and Bill's Muskie Club. Of the 700 muskies, only 25 were over the 30-pound mark. Less than four percent! Was it a bad year? Hardly. You can count the number of 40-pounders on one hand.

Telling it like it is—if the knowledgeable angler can't find the lunkers who can? The obvious conclusion is there simply aren't many trophies.

Muskie fishermen then have a choice. The sport can continue as is.

Stocking will help bolster the natural stock and everybody can stalk 30-inch muskies. The definition of a trophy will be revised downward. And we can all gather over a beer after a hard day of muskie fishing and yearn for the good old days.

Or. Muskie fishermen can unite to help bring back the good old days, to help insure that muskie fishing will forever be a quest for a legitimate trophy.

And they are doing just that.

Muskies, Inc., the nation's largest muskie organization, began emphasizing a muskie release program in 1970. Members preached to other members. The muskie is a trophy, not a meat fish. A muskie release awards program was started.

Other clubs have followed suit.

And what's happened? The results have been phenomenal. In 1975, Muskies, Inc. members caught 632 muskies and *released* 536 of them. In other words, 84 percent of the muskies that were fooled by a hook were released to be fooled again. Only they will be bigger muskies the next time.

Will a release program work? By all means.

The only question mark is: How much will the release program help the future of muskies? Of course not every released muskie will survive. And sincere fishermen will argue: Why let a 15-pounder go to die later when it could be used as food at least. True enough. Indeed some hooked muskies shouldn't be released if the fish obviously isn't going to survive.

Nevertheless, if only 10 out of 100 released muskies survive the ordeal of being caught, that's 10 more muskies alive and growing. Despite the uncertainties of the release program, one fact can't be disputed: If you stick that 15-pounder in the oven it is gone for sure. If released there's still a chance that it may one day be caught as a trophy.

Assume for a moment that every muskie released would survive. What are the returns? What does it mean?

Larry Ramsell, a Muskies, Inc., member and a strong advocate of the release program, took a look at the survival rate of stocked muskies. He then estimated how many 10- to 12-inch muskies had to be stocked to replace the adult muskies that are caught.

It's known, for example, that only about 94 out of 1,000 stocked muskie yearlings will survive and grow to reach 28 to 33 inches in length. In 1975 Muskies, Inc., members caught and released some 185 muskies that were 30 to 33 inches long. If those muskies had been kept instead, it would take a stocking of 1,968 yearlings and five to six years of waiting to replace the 185 fish.

Ramsell's data showed that for every muskie kept it takes 21 stocked muskies to replace it. If you wanted to replace one 47-inch muskie, you'd have to stock 143 yearling muskies, knowing only one would ever live long enough to reach 47 inches.

It should be clearly obvious that a muskie is worth too much to be caught only once.

But how many released muskies will survive? Nobody really knows. Ken Walker, a Wisconsin fisheries biologist, had handled hundreds of muskies during spawning operations. He is convinced that if a muskie is handled properly it will survive.

According to various studies of bass released after bass fishing tournaments, the survival rate may range between less than 10 percent and more than 90 percent. Why such a difference? Largely because there are proper and improper ways of handling a fish to be released.

Landing a Muskie

Before you can release (or keep) a muskie, it has to be landed, of course. (Assuming it fails to release itself.)

Although a muskie is most unpredictable before being hooked, it by no means follows any set pattern once it feels the barbs. I have seen muskies make absolutely spectacular leaps both immediately at the strike and throughout the battle. Or I've seen a hooked fish merely wallow and roll or pull half-heartedly against its unseen force, the fishing rod.

With a due respect, the muskie generally is credited with more fighting prowess than it normally exhibits. For its size, the muskie's endurance as a fighter is surprisingly short. But its combat fame is based on its explosiveness, either following the strike or when seeing the boat. Then anything can happen.

Following the strike and the setting of the hooks, it is best to reduce the drag on your reel. Changing the drag on an open-faced spinning reel can be cumbersome, since you must reach around with one hand and turn the knob on the face of the reel. As a result, most spinning reel users simply prefer to "back reel" to give line to a charging muskie. Back reeling can be dangerous, however, particularly if you lose your grip on the handle. The result of that usually is a nest of entangled monofilament and a lost muskie.

What do you do when the muskie leaps? Most muskie fishermen simply get a look of fear in their eyes. Sometimes the leap is done and over with before you can react. But if you can predict the leap, two methods are employed. Neither one is related. Some fishermen like to drop the rod toward the leaping fish. Others like to rear back on the leap in an attempt to knock the fish off its tail and back into the water. The differences in the techniques probably mean that there isn't much anybody can do to prevent the hooks from being thrown by a jumping muskie. Personally, I try to knock the muskie back down into the water. If anything, such manhandling might demoralize the muskie's will to leap again.

While the muskie has fresh strength, it is best to keep a fair distance. If need be, move the boat away from the fish. A fresh muskie on a short line is usually the one that escapes. As the muskie begins to tire—its runs will be shorter and less powerful—begin to shorten the line and draw the muskie within landing range.

If it's a muskie you intend to keep, some fishermen dispense with a landing net or gaff and simply apply the coup de grace with a club. Before striking the muskie, make sure the drag is light or the reel is free to give line. The blow may send the muskie on one final charge. If so, you want to be prepared to give line until you can ease the fish back to finish the job, if necessary.

If you're undecided about releasing or keeping the muskie, then a landing net or gaff is necessary. Most freshwater fishermen are not accustomed to the proper use of a gaff simply because it seldom is used, as compared to saltwater fishing. Hence the best landing tool is a muskie-sized net used properly. The muskie should always be taken from the head end. If a fish could swim backwards it might be different. By bringing the net from the head end, any muskie that tries a last-second charge will swim straight into the net.

However, don't hang the net in the water until the fish is ready to be netted. That's how nets get accidentally snagged by the lure while the muskie swims away. Once ready to net, sweep the net toward the muskie so the net is fully expanded by the drag in the water. And take the muskie dead center into the net. In that fashion, the muskie will be deep within the net before any hooks become entangled in the netting. Then in one complete motion close or pinch the top of the net against the side of the boat.

You now are in a position to dispatch or release the muskie. If it's a keeper, apply the coup de grace while the muskie is in the net and still outside of the boat. Never bring a live muskie onboard, regardless of what you intend to do with it, unless it is wrapped in a net.

Releasing a Muskie

Despite the serious reasons for releasing non-trophy muskies, there's irony and humor in the act. After you've worked so hard to get your hooks into a muskie, you may be faced with another difficult task: getting the hooks out.

The best way to free a muskie is very carefully. A slippery muskie with a mouthful of treble hooks is an accident waiting to happen. One careless slip and you could be hooked to the same lure. If that happens, you may have no other choice than to kill the muskie immediately to prevent it from flopping wildly, driving hooks deeper into your own flesh.

But there are ways to avoid such catastrophes, to safely release a muskie that will indeed have a chance of surviving.

One method is to avoid catching undersized muskies in the first place. If you see a small muskie follow—one that you know isn't a keeper you're looking for—try not to catch it. Stop the lure, don't complete a figure eight, wave your arms, stomp the boat—do anything to discourage the strike. Admittedly such tactics go against a fisherman's instincts. But the folks back home don't give ticker-tape parades for catching a boatload of 30-inch muskies. So—if you intend to release such a fish, why bother catching it?

Okay, the muskie is hooked and there's nothing more you can do about it, except remove the barbs. The tools you'll need are: a long-nosed pliers and possibly a sidecutter and a spring-steel clamp to hold the muskie's mouth open.

If possible, don't touch the muskie or lift it out of the water. Simply reach down with the pliers and remove the hooks while the muskie is still in the net. Keep the muskie in the water so that it remains calm. Hopefully.

If several hooks are hopelessly buried, take the sidecutters and cut the hooks as close to the muskie as possible. Don't tear the hooks free or you may be releasing a "dead" muskie.

If the muskie is small and you must hold it to remove the hooks, grab the muskie from above, gently placing your hand across the back behind the gill covers. Squeeze gently but firmly. Never grab a muskie by pinching the eyes. Once the muskie is firmly in hand you may then have to remove the net to get at the hooks.

When a muskie is too large to hold with one hand and the un-hooking chore is too difficult to complete while the fish is in the water, it's best to cut the hooks or lift the muskie onboard still in the net.

Once the hooks are removed, you must make the decision: Will the muskie live? If the muskie's gills or stomach is bleeding, the answer probably is no.

But seeing no serious tissue damage, it is reasonable to assume the muskie may well be suitable for release. If there's still a question, grab the muskie by the tail and pump the fish back and forth, forcing water through the muskie's gills. Piscatorial artificial respiration, if you will. Maintain the back-and-forth action until the muskie swims away under its own power. If the muskie is completely exhausted but breathing normally, the fish should be released in shallow water. Chances are it will be content to lie on the bottom until it regains its strength. A weak muskie released in deep water may sink to such depths that the water pressure will impede its ability to breathe.

It goes without saying that a muskie that is allowed to beat itself on the bottom of a boat or that is otherwise handled roughly will be a poor risk to survive.

If you've gone so far as to make the decision to release the muskie, you owe yourself the satisfaction that the muskie will indeed live.

Fisheries scientists have concluded that the reasons fish die after being released are: disease from excessive removal of the fish's protective mucus; internal injuries from improper handling; injury to the swim bladder from a rapid depth change; shock and stress from fighting or being held captive, and a lactic acid buildup in the muscular system from overexertion.

The physical damage to a muskie, such as bleeding gills, may be readily apparent. However, the problems of potentially fatal shock or lactic acid buildup cannot be diagnosed immediately. Hence, a muskie may appear perfectly healthy, although it may be destined to die a few days later.

The muskie fisherman can reduce those odds by releasing the muskie as soon as possible and by landing the muskie as soon as possible. The longer a muskie is needlessly "played in the water," the more exhausted it will become. A muskie that is subjected to a long "weigh-in" or photography session becomes a prime candidate for shock.

Of course you're interested in the size of the muskie, even if you intend to release it. The quickest and easiest method to measure a muskie is to mark off known distances on the side of your boat. In that manner, the muskie will never have to leave the water but you'll still know its length. And from the length you can obtain a ballpark weight guesstimate.

Releasing Thyself

May you never have to face a treble (or single) hook that is buried in your own flesh. Discounting minor pricks and jabs, I have, on one occasion, stared in disbelief at my thumb, which was adorned with a muskie-sized treble hook. One barb was well buried. Dead center.

Now as a former biology student, I have dissected everything from white-tailed deer vaginas to preserved farm cats. I've skinned my share of squirrels and fileted a fish or two. But when I saw my poor defenseless thumb, a cold sweat spread across my colorless face. My knees began to weaken and my strength was drained. You'd have thought I had just bottled my own blood.

Fortunately my fishing partner was not so incapacitated. He poured a little bourbon on the wound and deftly yanked the hook out.

A medical doctor might shudder at my partner's methods but we had no choice. Professional medical attention simply wasn't available.

Most medical experts recommend pushing the hook through, if possible, to expose the barb. Then cut the barb off and retract the hook.

Still another method is to tie a strong line or cord at the bend of the hook, push down on the eye of the hook, then give a sharp, strong yank on the cord, pulling the hook out from the same direction it entered. The open wound then should be washed with a disinfectant if available. At the very least wash the wound in clean water.

Basically that's the technique my partner applied. Except he used a pliers with good booze as a disinfectant.

I never asked what brand.

A Final Reflection

Some fishermen have so wanted to catch a big muskie they've prayed that it might happen. Others less desperate have not yet sought such High Authority.

But it's doubtful if the Creator will intervene. The mechanics of making trophy muskies have been supplied. There is water and food and a fish that is willing to eat and grow. And there are fishermen to indulge in the wonder of it all.

But unfortunately we've really never learned to appreciate with much restraint. Our forefathers marveled at the vast forests and sweeping prairies and then proceeded to cut and plow them away.

The magnificent muskellunge received no better treatment.

But that has changed and will change. More muskie fishermen will discover that their own act of restraint—to release a muskie—is the only long-lasting, meaningful reward. That the gratification in the sport of fishing comes not from what you take but what you give to maintain it.

In that sense, you can answer your own prayers.

Part IV

The M.I. Story

If you've fished for muskies; if you think you'll fish for muskies; or even if you don't fish at all: remember the name—Muskies, Incorporated.

There are hundreds of sportsmen's organizations. A list would be a mile long. And Muskies, Incorporated, would be included under the cold definition of "fishing clubs."

But Muskies, Incorporated, is more than that.

It is a Cinderella story not found in fairy tales.

It is the hope of fishermen with unselfish dreams.

It is a product of determination, inspired by the human spirit.

Muskies, Inc., is all of these things, but the story doesn't end there. Nor is it complete. Its growth and achievements are not yet done. Its concern for the mighty muskellunge has not waned. There is more to do. And there always will be.

Muskie fishermen haven't learned the meaning of surrender. The test is the muskie itself. Those who fail switch to a fish that makes sense.

But therein lies the strength of Muskies, Inc., a deep dedication that has led to renewed interest in the welfare of the muskie. A concern that inspired the acquisition of its own muskie hatchery and initiated a fish-for-fun, muskie-release program that is practiced by hundreds of its members.

What's more, it all started in the mind of one man. An extraordinary human being. His name is Gilbert C. Hamm. He lives in St. Paul, Minnesota. He is president of his own building construction firm. Successful. Smart. Gregarious. He thrives on work. Accomplishments. He's an expert pottery maker, self-taught. Not halfway. He's read every book ever published on pottery-making. Some of them twice. Every glaze recipe is meticulously recorded, filed away for future reference.

He's curious, inventive, ambitious. His friends call him "Gil."

He's a positive thinker. If something needs to be done, then do it. But do it right. Gil Hamm has no time for wasted energy. Doesn't believe in it.

He's an organizer. An entrepreneur. He's spent a lifetime making liars out of those who said it couldn't be done.

How such a man also became a muskie fishing enthusiast only fate can explain.

Gil Hamm and his wife were en route to fish muskies, appropriately enough, when a thought crossed his mind. He and his wife were Minnesotans, land of 10,000 lakes and sky-blue waters. But they were headed for Canada to chase muskies. And they were not alone. Many carloads of other fishermen, bearing Minnesota license plates, were also crossing the border. Some to pursue muskies.

There was no thunder and lightning but the irony struck Hamm. Why was it necessary to leave such a water-rich state to fish for muskies? He knew the answer. Minnesota's native muskie populations were considered luxuries. The bread-and-butter fishes—the species that received the attention of fish managers—were walleyes and northern pike.

Gil Hamm had made up his mind. On the return trip home, while his wife drove the car, Hamm sat with his ever-present pocket notebook and turned an idea into an organizational chart: For a muskie club.

He envisioned a club that would help raise and stock muskies for Minnesota. His logic was simple. If the muskie needed help, the muskie fisherman would have to provide it.

Gil Hamm returned home a restless man. He felt his idea was solid.

Who could object to the motives: Muskie fishermen spending their own time and money to improve their own sport.

But Gil Hamm was in for a surprise. Some thought his idea was interesting but kooky. He revealed his dream to state fisheries officials. They said it would never work. One official said if Hamm was so interested in muskies he ought to fish in Wisconsin.

The pessimism and the defeatist attitudes merely served to fuel Hamm's determination. The pessimists were right. The road would be long and rough. But they hadn't met a Gil Hamm before.

In December of 1966—at the age of 62—Gil Hamm was charged and ready to act. On a Friday evening, the 9th, Hamm invited some fellow muskie enthusiasts to a meeting in an upstairs room over the Criterion Cafe in St. Paul.

Fourteen fishermen showed up. They kicked around some ideas. They asked why. Why can't the muskie be an attraction in Minnesota? Why can't more be done for a fish that, by all standards, is the greatest trophy in fresh water?

They agreed to meet again the next month in Minneapolis at the Minnesota Press Club. Membership was left open; no dues were set. However, officers were elected in that first meeting. Bud Meier was named vice-president, Eric Rehnwall secretary and Rod Guindon treasurer. All others in attendance were members of the Board of Directors, automatically.

Of course Gil Hamm was voted president. About that there was no question. There also was no question that with Gil Hamm at the helm, Muskies, Incorporated, was not about to wither and blow away. The only thing that ever crumbled in Hamm's hand was a bad piece of pottery.

At an age when most men start to slow down, Hamm was locked into a new venture. He went everywhere, visiting muskie experts in Wisconsin, corresponding with biologists elsewhere. He surrounded himself with other fishermen with ambition. Their rabid interest in the muskie made the news and their timing was uncanny.

By coincidence, a civic group in Battle Lake, Minnesota, had experimented with raising muskies in a private fish hatchery owned by Darrell Trumbauer.

Hamm needed no coaching. Only months after Muskies, Inc., was founded, arrangements had been made with Trumbauer to use his hatchery facilities to raise muskies. Trumbauer was a skilled fish culturist, a man familiar with the ins and outs of raising suckers for bait shops. Only now those valuable forage fish would be fed to muskies. And they were about to arrive. Some 300 muskies—each about three inches long—were purchased from a hatchery in Wisconsin.

Muskies, Inc., was not even a year old.

Also in 1967 the fledgling organization made its first stocking of 100 yearling muskies in Sugar Lake in Wright County. Meanwhile, the original membership of 14 was increasing by leaps and bounds. By the time Muskies, Inc., reached its second birthday there were 400 members in the fold.

Not that there weren't setbacks. Muskies, Inc., had launched projects along many fronts, political as well as biological. They found it was easier to catch muskies than sway politicians. Muskies, Inc., backed bills in Minnesota's legislature that would ban spearing. They argued that spearing was an unsportsmanlike method of taking fish; they argued that muskies were being illegally speared even though the fish was not a legal target.

They lost the argument. But they won a concession. More Minnesota lakes would be added to the list of "designated muskie waters" where spearing would be prohibited.

However, Hamm and his growing collection of fellow muskie addicts also were impatient and unsatisfied with the limited muskie program of Minnesota's Department of Natural Resources. There were personality conflicts and differences of opinion over priorities. In short, Muskies, Inc., and the state fisheries officials had a cool relationship at the start. But understanding eventually prevailed.

To help Muskies, Inc., launch its hatchery operation, Minnesota lent muskies to raise with the understanding that the lakes to be stocked would be selected by the state. Petty differences were replaced by a spirit of cooperation.

Meanwhile Muskies, Inc., continued to grow and expand its horizons.

An "International" muskie fishing tournament was sponsored in 1968. Thirty-seven contestants showed up. Four years later the event would attract 375 anglers. And by 1975 more than 600 fishermen from throughout the country would participate in the annual September happening.

But these were not tournaments to kill muskies. If a contestant caught a fish that was worth the wall, it was kept. But otherwise the tournament emphasized competition to see which fisherman could release the most muskies.

The tournament wasn't held in Wisconsin or Canada. No way. Gil Hamm was out to deliver a message: Muskies also could attract fishermen tourists to Minnesota to help bolster one of the state's biggest industries. There was good muskie fishing in Minnesota. The tournaments would show that. And Muskies, Inc., was intent on making that fishing better. Then Hamm and his cohorts dropped another bombshell. For every fisherman entered in the 1975 tournament, a yearling muskie would be stocked in the tournament lake of the angler's choice. Such infamous waters as Leech Lake, Cass Lake, Winnibigoshish and several others. The same waters Gil Hamm had driven by on that muskie fishing trip in 1966.

The membership list continued to grow. Other innovative ideas were put to work. Arrangements were made with the Gold Bond Stamp Company, a national firm based in Minneapolis, to add another "gift" in exchange for the trading stamps. That gift: a muskie to be donated to Muskies, Inc.

Trapshoots, prize drawings, raffles, sponsor programs—every possible, and some impossible, fund-raising projects were launched. Muskies, Inc., obtained national publicity in the sporting magazines. Hamm once guided the two popular stars of television's *Gunsmoke*, Milburn ("Doc") Stone and Ken ("Festus") Curtis on a muskie fishing trip. Their adventures were filmed for later showing on *The American Sportsman*, a national network series. The two cowboy heroes caught muskies, too.

Agreements were worked out with local Minnesota sportsmen's groups to underwrite the cost of young muskies from Muskies, Inc., for stocking in their area lakes.

Corporations and private donors chipped in thousands of dollars to further realize the organization's goals. The members themselves—from all walks of life: bankers and store clerks, doctors and truck drivers—would gather for work sessions, building nets, draining ponds, hauling fish. All volunteer help.

Four years after he started, Gil Hamm figured his "baby" had grown enough. It was time for him to step down as president "and let some younger boys in there." He would remain an officer, however.

But suddenly Muskies, Inc., no longer was exclusively a Minnesota product. The organization's enthusiasm had been carried away by out-of-state fishermen as well. New Muskies, Inc., chapters began springing up in other states—North Dakota, Illinois, Missouri, Wisconsin.

Its membership had increased to over 2,000 fishermen from more than 22 states and a couple of foreign countries.

The muskie hatchery in Battle Lake was purchased by Muskies, Inc., and expanded. Trumbauer was hired to run what had become an $80,000 facility. He was the first paid employee.

In 1976 Muskies, Inc., announced its plans to ship muskies to lakes outside of Minnesota. The possibility of a second muskie hatchery was explored.

Indeed Muskies, Inc., had taken the first step toward leading a national drive for the betterment of muskie fishing.

A step that even Gil Hamm had not envisioned. The organization's original goal was to develop 800 to 1,000 muskie lakes in Minnesota. Pure and simple. And the job would be done. But the muskie movement has since become much broader, including scientific muskie research and tagging projects.

The goal for Minnesota still is far from being completed. But it's not bogged down, either. And Hamm is not worried. "I may not see it but we'll reach 1,000 lakes. But I'm gonna be around for most of them. Let me tell you, I've had lots of help."

Indeed. One man may start a movement but no man keeps it going alone. With Hamm, there was Bob Hill, Ed Peterka, Frank Schneider, Bob Shoop, Pete Hadley, Xen Stoner, Hugh Becker, Helen Ness, Tom Fudally, Mark Windels, George Keller, Vince Rakow, Frank Steger, Lou Cook, George Selcke, Elmo Korn, Jim Randash, Larry Ramsell, Larry Porter, Jim Peterson, Dr. Gerald Jurgens, Gary Bennyhoff, Tom Meyers, Greg Ohman, Bob Zempel, Bud Gustafson, Mike Stoner, Jerry Sundboom, Dr. Chan Cotton, Les Kouba, Dick Chapman, Bud Meier, Dr. Charles Huver, Ray Ostrom, Stan Kumpula, Marty Engle, Ed Scholten, Burt Pelkey, Rod Guindon, C. L. Weyerhauser, Charlie Welf, John Uldrich, Bob Farinacci, Don Bloese, Ken Haag, Gary Myhre, Al Skaar, Maynard Olson, Richard Ruhl, Roy Plankers, and many more.

However, the unsung contributors to Muskies, Inc., are the muskie fishing members who not only formulated the organization's principles but also practiced them. Here those principles are:

Purposes of Muskies, Incorporated
1708 University Ave., St. Paul, Minn. 55104

To promote a high quality muskellunge sport fishery;
To support selected conservation practices based on scientific merit as carried out by authorized federal and state agencies;
To promote muskellunge research, establishment of hatcheries and introduction of the species into suitable waters;
To support the abatement of water pollution;
To provide a library facility for scientific and popular muskellunge literature, and to maintain records of habits, growth and range of the species;
To disseminate muskellunge information;
To promote good fellowship and sportsmanship among men, women and children.

But as a collective body, Muskies, Inc., members also went forth preaching a new gospel: Release Your Muskies. Then they set an example. Fishing for fun. Releasing their muskies. Each united in a common bond to make muskie fishing truly a trophy hunt. A hunt that someday could be fulfilled if the smaller muskies were allowed to live and grow.

The organization's commitment to the release ethic is staggering. Consider the results of their members fishing contest from 1970 to 1975:

Year	Muskies Caught	Kept	Released	Percent Released
1970	58	47	11	19 %
1971	96	66	30	31
1972	164	69	95	58
1973	272	63	209	77
1974	283	50	233	82
1975	632	96	536	85

In their 1975 International Tournament, involving members and non-members, a total of 38 muskies were caught in the three-day event. But only seven muskies were kept and 31 (or nearly 82 percent) were returned alive.

In the same five-year span, the largest muskies to be caught and set free measured 50 inches! Not one but two!

But the most phenomenal catch and release achievement was made in 1975 by a retired veterinarian and Muskies, Inc., member, Dr. Chan Cotton. In one summer season, the Minnesotan hooked and landed 108 legal-sized muskies. And he released 107! All witnessed. The one fish that was kept had accidentally been killed. The largest muskie he released was 49 inches long, between 35 and 30 pounds.

In the meantime Muskies, Inc., kept laying the foundation for the future: muskie stocking. With the cooperation of Minnesota's Department of Natural Resources, who provided thousands of muskie fry on a coop basis, Muskies, Inc., raised and released more than 27,000 yearling muskies.

That does not count some 25 keeper-sized muskies that were released in the St. Croix River. Not long after the tagged muskies were set free, an 82-year-old river fisherman pulled out the surprise of his life. A 33-inch, seven-pound muskie. The old angler was ecstatic.

"That muskie proved I ain't dead yet," he quipped.

Gil Hamm can say the same thing about his dream—Muskies, Inc.

Part V

Talking with the Muskie Masters

Ted Capra

Most fishermen hone their angling skills on panfish, bass or other finned targets before graduating to the elusive muskie.

Ted Capra was not so ordinary. He jumped in feet-first. The muskie was his first attraction. While he has gone on to become skilled as an all-around angler, the Minnesotan earned his stripes and recognition as a relentless chaser of muskies.

By the time he was 37 years old, Capra already had spent 15 seasons hunting muskies. His largest went 36½ pounds. He's landed several over 30 and many over 20. In fact, his best single day of muskie fishing produced three muskies, each over 20 pounds. That's more muskie poundage than some less fortunate anglers take in a lifetime.

Capra speaks:

About muskie lakes: "If I was going into an area that was new and I had never fished it before, I would try and get a little history of the lakes. Then I would get a map and find the sunken islands. These are my key spots. Any sunken islands with weed growth on top are probably the number-one muskie spots. Weed lines with points sticking out, protruding far out into the lake, are normally good spots, mainly the cabbage (pondweed) beds.

157

"There are lakes that have weedbeds all the way around the whole lake. So you can start from one end and fish the whole lake. The key areas would be sunken islands, points protruding out into the lake. Normally wherever there is good walleye fishing, it will be a point or a sunken island. There are muskies around there feeding on those walleyes.

"The more I fish, the more I am finding out about bare rock humps out in the middle of the lake, especially in Minnesota and Canada. These little humps sitting out in the middle of the lakes may hold big muskies. On a rock hump within the first 10 to 15 minutes you will know if there are muskies there. Then you can leave and constantly come back. Those fish will be there sometime during the day.

"I've got a point on one of my favorite lakes where the muskies come in, although it is quite a distance from deep water. Then in another lake, there is deep water within 20 feet. In other words, it is a real steep hump and there is deep water close by. But I don't believe that deep water is necessary. On another lake there are two blocks of boulders before you get into any deep water at all and the deepest water is about 18 feet. So you are fishing a flat with boulders and there are many times when it holds muskies. So we are really talking about weedbeds and rock piles."

About favorite fishing times and why: "Well, I like to fish during the middle of the day, believe it or not. I'd say I've caught more muskies during the middle of the day between say 10 and 3. I believe that in the morning, especially in the middle of the summer, muskies are not in the weedbeds. Or if they are, they are not active. And I believe that's the case because of a lack of oxygen in the weeds early in the morning. In other words weeds give off oxygen during the day, but take it away at night. So early in the morning the muskies aren't there and there are no bait fish there. As the weeds give off oxygen, the bait fish move in and the muskies move in and feed on them. And this is the reason I like midday. Now there are a lot of muskies caught at 6 in the morning and at 8 at night. But I think, overall, more fish have been caught during midday. I just think it is the most productive time."

About lures: "It depends on the time of the year. Early in the spring I find that jigs and small spinners seem to work better than the bigger normal muskie lures that people would know as a muskie lure. In other words, walleye jigs with a little wire leader so that you don't get cut off. Little crank baits, bass lures, seem to be effective early in the spring. As you go into summer, from the middle of June on, then I go to bigger lures. I like jerk baits the best, such as Suick, Eddy Baits, Teddy Baits and Bobbie Baits. I found these to be very effective for big muskies. Bucktails, such as Mepps and Worth, are good for taking muskies, but I have never taken any big muskies on these particular lures. I like the diving plugs, such as the Rapala and the Cisco Kid, which have a tight wiggle that will dive down depending on how far you cast it. You can get down to about 10 to 12 feet. I like working them along the weed lines."

About fishing gear, rods, reels, and terminal tackle: "I have several different rods, not really to fight the fish but to make the lures work properly. I use a fairly stiff action rod for jerk baits and also the steady retrieve baits. Bucktail, I go to a little lighter rod. You can cast it a lot farther and there is a little more feel to it. I have been using bait cast reels. As far as how important the terminal tackle is, everyone has their own opinion on it, but I'll give you an example. I know a guy that throws a 50-pound test line and catches as many muskies as I do, and I use a monofilament, so everybody has different ideas. I don't think it is as important as people make it out to be because the fish is really not the greatest fighter. The trick is to make them strike and after you got the initial set you could land them on an eight-pound test line."

About mistakes unsuccessful muskie fishermen make: "I have heard a lot of guys say they have been muskie fishing for 12 years and never got one. But they go out and probably work for an hour and that is the extent of their muskie fishing. I think one of the mistakes that people make when they go out muskie fishing is that they are not in the right frame of mind. They go out thinking they are going to get blanked because they are muskie fishing. Positive thinking plays a big part, as far as I am concerned, in taking muskies. If you think you are not going to get a fish then you won't. Normally when a guy goes out to start muskie fishing, he doesn't know where to go, what to do. That is probably the biggest fault of the inexperienced muskie fisherman. Not knowing where to go."

About the single most important factor in catching muskies: "Confidence. No one really talks about confidence as much as I put an emphasis on it. But I believe that confidence really plays a very big role in taking muskies. Everybody normally goes for the same spots but some people catch more fish than others and I think it's concentration on making the lure work right. In other words, you have to put action into the lure. This is one of the most important things. Imagine if you are using a lure that looks like an injured minnow, try to make it look like an injured minnow. That is probably the most important thing that I can think of."

Why is he a good muskie fisherman?

"I think it is because I am stubborn. I go out and work hard at it. It is really an endurance test. Although I have learned more and more, it is not unusual to go out and take a couple of muskies a day. I think it is because of knowledge and endurance, really. Just sitting out there and waiting for that moment to happen. And being there when it does."

Mark Windels

Before Mark Windels reached his 30th birthday, he'd proven that youth is no handicap in taking muskies. Within five years, Windels had caught 79 legal-sized muskies, including four over 30 pounds. In addition, he's released 49-inchers and 32-pounders, believing that a fish-for-fun ethic is the best way of preserving muskie fishing for yourself and others.

Yet Windels is an aggressive fisherman who fishes hard and thinks hard. He, too, has invented his own lure, a bucktail called the Harasser.

Windels speaks:

About muskie lakes: "I pay particular attention to the weeds, the cabbage-type weeds, located on large food shelves with access to deep water. Generally, I'm talking about sunken islands and bars with the right type of vegetation, dropping into deep water. Many fishermen relate to the necessity of deep water but often they do not consider the necessity of food shelves. The food has to be there to attract the muskie in the first place."

About favorite fishing times and why: "The time of the year would be fall—September and October, primarily—because the larger muskies tend to move into shallow water where they are more vulnerable to presently used fishing methods. For time of day, I prefer fishing evenings. However, I try and not limit myself to fishing any certain time of day. I usually commit myself to fishing the entire day—and the entire season, for that matter. To get a muskie means fishing some of the tough days plus the good days. You just have to get out there and put your time in and take your fish when they come."

About lures: "My first choice is a bucktail spinner—of course my own, Harasser. My second choice would probably be a type of jerk bait, such as Suick. My third choice would be a diving plug, such as Cisco Kid."

About fishing gear, rods, reels, and terminal tackle: "I feel there is no substitute for quality tackle; I go first class. You have to pay considerable attention to it and keep it in top-notch condition. It's almost a must to start with quality tackle in the first place. I use a six-foot heavy-duty muskie rod. It is a very stiff rod, which gives me backbone to work a jerk bait and enough backbone to set the hook solidly and quickly. I always use a wire leader, about 60-pound, snap and swivel. I generally use a 36-pound Dacron test line."

About mistakes unsuccessful muskie fishermen make: "They do not pay enough attention to their terminal tackle. Weak links. They tend to use lures that are on the market with poor quality hooks or are put together in a fashion that will not hold up. I think almost all of the tackle in the market can stand some improvement, in terms of the quality hooks, the ways the screw eyes are put in, the quality of split rings used. First of all, one should not just trust something because it comes from a tackle shop. You should check out the construction. A fisherman often underestimates the quality of their tackle and then when it comes to getting a big fish on, it is generally due to tackle failure that he loses it. Another reason I have been somewhat successful is that I tend to fish prime muskie water. The fisherman who wants to catch a muskie should go to prime muskie water, he should find out where fish are being caught in rather good numbers, and concentrate on that water. By fishing somewhat marginal waters you are somewhat handicapping yourself."

About the single most important factor in catching a muskie: "Location of the fish. That takes two forms. First, you have to locate the right lake, fish prime waters. Second, you have to locate the spot on the lake where the fish are commonly taken. A good spot on the lake will keep producing good muskies, year after year. You should spend time on location. It is the prime factor."

Why is he a good muskie fisherman?

"I do some research on muskie fishing, finding out what is prime water. I spend my time on the water to learn that water well. By learning where the fish are commonly taken and spending time on the water, you eventually connect with fish. Again it's paying your dues, learning as much as you can. Experience pays off. The more knowledge you have about the fish, the more readily you can catch it.

"Confidence is very important. You have to have confidence in the lake you are fishing, the lure you are fishing with. It keeps you fishing hard and it keeps you alert. By first selecting prime muskie waters and using your favorite lure you are already fishing with confidence. The only thing that can get you down is the weather. Confidence is important but you build your own confidence by using the right water and lure, and fishing hard."

Chan "Doc" Cotton

Somebody forgot to tell Chan "Doc" Cotton that muskie fishing is supposed to be tough. He makes it look easy. A retired veterinarian, Doc Cotton lives on the shores of Minnesota's Leech Lake. He was in his early forties before he discovered the fish. And in that first season he landed one legal muskie. His second season he caught three or four. Then after only two years of muskie fishing experience, Doc Cotton caught an unbelievable 108 muskies—all legal-sized—in his third season, 124 days. And he released 107. He accomplished his feat by hard work, hard study and hard desire.

Cotton speaks:

About muskie lakes: "Where I look first for muskies depends on the time of the year. But primarily I'm a weed fisherman. I prefer the cabbage. If there isn't any cabbage or lunge weed then I go for the bulrushes or cattails. In the spring I start shallow and then move deeper as the summer progresses. In the fall I look for rocks, boulders and sandbars. Since I cast most of the time, rather than troll, I look for deep water near the weedbeds."

About favorite fishing times and why: "My favorite time is around 9 A.M. in the morning. We (his wife, Betty, is a constant fishing companion) have caught most of our fish then and that is why it is our favorite. I don't know why. In the spring our best luck is between noon and 4 P.M. I don't have any answers for that either. Maybe it's the angle of the sun's rays. Yet my favorite months are July, September and October."

About lures: "Mepps has been, by far, the most effective lure, the giant killer with a black bucktail and the rainbow finish on the blade. The diving Cisco Kid with a perch finish would be my second choice. But I think it's important to retrieve the bucktail lure as fast as possible. At least that's been the most productive for me."

About fishing gear, rods, reels and terminal tackle: "I think terminal tackle is mighty important. Not so with rods and reels. The best is what a person gets used to. But with terminal tackle I get a little fussy, since I have lost a few fish. That's why I use a steel leader. I've had muskie cut monofilament three different times. So I went back to a leader, coated braided wire of about 45-pound test. For fishing line I use about 30-pound test monofilament."

About mistakes unsuccessful muskie fishermen make: "I think number one is lack of confidence. When I go out there I am sure that I'm going to catch at least one fish. I am positive. And I fire myself up for it.

"But also I think too many fishermen come up to a weedbed or rock pile the wrong way. I try to approach as quietly as possible. I rarely fish with the motor running, especially if I'm fishing in clear water."

About the single most important factor in catching muskies: "Well, I'd again say confidence, and then, knowing the lakes or rivers, the waters you are fishing. If you don't know the muskie haunts, finding one is a highly difficult task."

Why is he a good muskie fisherman?

"Well, I've been fishing something all my life. But my dad always taught me, 'If you're gonna do something do it the best, try to be Number One.' So I work at my muskie fishing and I read everything I can."

Homer LeBlanc

Homer LeBlanc remembers his first muskie fishing trip. It was with his grandfather. LeBlanc was six years old. Since then, LeBlanc has been chasing muskies on Michigan's Lake St. Clair for more than a half century. He is a trolling fisherman exclusively, having pioneered many techniques as well as inventing trolling-type lures, such as the Swim Whiz.

In that time, LeBlanc has boated some 3,000 muskies and taught hundreds of fishermen his trolling know-how.

LeBlank speaks:

About muskie lakes: "I know Lake St. Clair so well, that is the only lake I fish. However, if I was going to go to a strange lake I would look for points of land and where weedbeds might be. I fish the depths of 10 to 18 feet near drop-offs. That is the important thing."

About favorite fishing times and why: "If I had only an hour to fish it would be between 1:30 and 2:30 in the afternoon. That is my best one-hour period. For a four-hour period, from 11 A.M. to 3 P.M. is really it. In our muskie club, 70 percent of the muskies are caught between the hours of 11 A.M. and 3 P.M.

"June, July and August are my best months. When you get into late August and early September there is a three-week lull, the dog days. Then from about September 20th on, it gets really good. The month of October is fantastic but you run into a lot of bad weather. October and November is when the lunkers come in."

About lures: "I haven't fished with anything except Homer LeBlanc lures since 1952, the Swim Zag and the Swim Whiz lure. They are still my favorite lures and they are the ones that are catching the majority of the muskies. I can't fish with other equipment other than my own. It just wouldn't feel right."

About fishing gear, rods, reels and terminal tackle: "Well, that's the most important thing. There are a lot of fellas on the lake that fish with monofilament leaders but I just can't go for that. With monofilament leaders, they are just risking losing a big fish. You know it doesn't make sense. So my leaders are made of wire. Most any rod and reel will do the trick. The thing is to keep your hook sharp and have good snaps and swivels; you can't have that junk that will break. You can't use cheap snaps and swivels."

About mistakes unsuccessful muskie fishermen make: "The biggest mistake they make is not having enough drag on the reel to hook a fish. They fish with their rods in the holders. Then, they don't release some of that drag. They have a tight drag on and then hustle that fish to the boat as fast as they can. The quicker you get them to the boat and try to land them the easier it is to lose them. That is the one mistake that amateurs make. When we get a fish on, I take some of the drag off of the reel and I don't care how much line he is going to take out, I'll take the boat back to him if necessary. I thought we had the world record on the other day. A fish struck the lure and hooked himself in the tail. He took about 125 yards of line without a stop. So I stopped the forward motion of the boat and started to go back. Finally we started getting near where we could get him in the boat. We saw we had him hooked by the tail, but we really thought we had the world record on."

About the single most important factor in catching a muskie: "Well, fooling a muskie. You catch more muskies fooling them than you will just throwing the lure in the water. The one factor that catches muskies more than anything is churning water. That is, churned up with your propeller. Muskies associate churning water with possibly being live bait and minnows. The result is that muskies see a lure close to the boat. By close, I mean they see a lure about four feet off the corner of the boat on each side and about two feet down below the surface of the water. About 65 percent of the muskies caught are caught on those two rods. Then I will fish one back in the center in the wash about five or six feet down and about 15 feet from the boat. That is another big producer. Another thing that fools a muskie is when letting out a lure. If I am going to let a lure out about 35 feet or so I let the lure drop. I put it in the water and then let the lure drop for about 10 feet, stop it and let it work again. As the lure levels off I'll let it drop again. If a muskie happens to see that lure dropping he is not about to let it go, he's going to grab."

Why is he a good muskie fisherman?

"I am a good muskie fisherman because I specialize in it. I've tried different methods, but my method of fishing catches fish. Keep them lures close to the boat. The old-time guys used to fish three lines and let them out 75 to 100 feet to the back of the boat. They would have those three lines fouled up all the time. Now I successfully fish eight rods all the time. I don't have any of them more than 30 to 35 feet out."

Larry Ramsell

Larry Ramsell is the epitome of the muskie addict. A resident of Galesburg, Illinois, he does not have muskie waters nearby but that hasn't cooled his enthusiasm for the fish. He's chased muskies for more than 25 years but his zeal has not ebbed. Ramsell reads everything about muskies, tries everything and even writes about the fish. In addition, he's the official world records secretary for the Freshwater Fishing Hall of Fame. Strictly a caster, Ramsell has caught muskies up to 30 pounds.

Ramsell speaks:

About muskie lakes: "It depends a lot on the type of lake. I try to limit my fishing area to just trophy fishing. I've caught as many small ones as I like to catch. I don't want to catch too many small ones because you do take a chance on killing a small one whenever you hook it. I fish trophy fish waters. My idea of what trophy fish waters are may not coincide with a lot of people, but they've got to have some deep water. There has to be food, of course, or the muskies wouldn't be there. I like the underwater reefs and deep-edge weedbeds. If you find the two in combination, so much the better.

"I haven't had that much luck with points. Whenever I can find an underwater reef with the weeds somewhere nearby and deep water close by, I know I have got a trophy fish spot. Then, it's just a matter of putting in your time and paying your dues. I had such a spot for six years before I ever saw a fish there. But when the muskies started it seemed like they just didn't shut off. We caught four fish there the first year and they were all over 22 pounds."

About favorite fishing time and why: "I have had the best luck in the evenings. I have caught my biggest fish in the evenings. Not night fishing, but after supper until dark. The 30-pounder that I caught was at 9 o'clock. I see some big fish in the daytime also but they seem more willing to do business in the evening.

"I personally feel a good muskie fisherman will have to pay his dues. In the middle of summer or in the fall. You can find big fish anytime. There is no doubt that the best fishing is in the fall, it's been proven over the years and I wouldn't argue with it a bit. Muskies are harder to find in midsummer, I would say. You keep reading reports that there are fish being caught but I have to believe that this is due to the great number of anglers pounding the water. Consequently if a big fish decides to move, somebody is going to be there with the bait. In the fall you have a lot less people fishing but yet you still seem to see a goodly number of fish. If I had my druthers I would probably spend the last two weeks in September and the first week in October really doing some serious trophy hunting."

About lures: "There is no doubt that the bucktail is the all-time greatest muskie lure. But there is no doubt that it is used the most. It is effective in hooking fish; even the novice can take it out and work it properly. When a fish hits, they have maximum opportunity to set the hooks. I have had tremendous amounts of luck with jerk baits. It depends on how you use them. They are a lot of work, but they will move a lot of fish. You can catch fish with jerk baits when nothing else will work."

About fishing gear, rods, reels, and terminal tackle: "I personally use the best that money will buy. It may not be the most expensive, but it is the most solid. I've got perhaps half a dozen different rods. You have got to have some backbone in a rod, there is no doubt about it. You've got to be able to drive those hooks into that bony jaw. If you don't you are just kidding yourself. For hook setting, Dacron line is my preference. Usually around 36-pound class.

I always use a steel leader. I make my own."

About mistakes unsuccessful muskie fishermen make: "I believe in the figure eight. Everybody muskie fishing should watch their bait—not necessarily the bait, but behind and below their bait—and see those fish coming before it is too late. Keep the bait moving. Once the bait makes the hesitation the fish is gone.

"You wouldn't believe how many fish we catch at the boat. It is not really the hardest place to catch them. I keep a light drag. All you have to do is let them take off. The battle is half over right there.

"I caught a 50-incher last year. The fish was probably about 30 feet from the boat when it hit. The first thing a muskie does usually is jump. People say big fish don't jump, but that is not true. I have never seen one that didn't either jump or come halfway out of the water and shake that bait. The first thing I do is stick that rod right in the water down to the reel and pull him right back into the water. If you see the line coming up fast, jam your rod down. If you can keep them down, you can catch them. If they jump, there is nothing you can do about it.

"It's hard to dump a big muskie, but at least you are keeping that hook tight. A lot of times the hook isn't really buried yet when they make the first jump. If you don't keep tension on the line the minute you give him slack, that bait is going to fly right over your head. In fact I lost one last year about 35 pounds, it came out so fast I didn't have time to set again and the bait just about hit me in the ear. If you don't keep tension on it they are going to get rid of it."

About the single most important factor in catching a muskie: "The first thing you've got to do is find them. For trophy hunting you have got to pay your dues, like I said before. You have got to locate the fish and you have to stay with him. You wouldn't believe how many fish we catch with the figure eight. The critical time is not when the fish is at the boat, it's before it gets there. Usually you can see it coming unless it is really windy and there's a bad glare on the water. I always wear Polaroids and keep my hat pulled down low so I have got maximum visibility under the water. If I can see those fish coming and keep that bait moving I've got a better chance. Usually in the fall they will hit a figure eight better than in the summer. But it seems like the big fish have the worst habit of following right up to the boat. They are the fish that are grabbing the figure eight the most often.

"You've got to feel that you are on a muskie spot or there isn't any use being there. Every day I go out I try and work in at least half a dozen new spots. If I've got confidence I am going to see fish. If you don't have confidence the first thing you do is not pay attention to your bait. You don't see the fish and consequently you feel like there is no fish there."

Why is he a good muskie fisherman?

"I fish only for muskies. Not because I don't like to fish for other species. Where I live the fishing is very limited, I spend all my vacation time and all my weekend trips going for muskies. I live and breathe muskies. I am regional vice-president for Muskies, Incorporated. I learn everything I can about them. I learn from the bass fisherman because these are the people doing the most research right now. But everything they learn can be applied to muskie fishing. You have to keep constantly on the alert. You have to be thinking all the time. You don't just go out there and throw a bait and reel it back in."

Appendix

State-by-State Survey of Muskie Waters

State	Top Muskie Waters
Alabama	Tennessee River
Alaska	None
Arizona	None (Stocking attempts have failed.)
Arkansas	None
California	None
Colorado	None
Connecticut	None
Delaware	None
Florida	None
Georgia	None
Hawaii	None
Idaho	None
Illinois	Spring Lake, Shabana, Chain of Lakes (None stocked earlier than 1975.)
Indiana	Brookville Reservoir (stocked in 1974), Whitewater River and Tributaries
Iowa	West Okoboji, Clear Lake

Kansas	None
Kentucky	Cave Run Lake, Licking River, Beaver Creek, Green River, Red River, Kinniconick Creek, Tygarts Creek, Barren River, Ohio River.
Louisiana	None
Maine	None
Maryland	None (Few caught in Susquehanna River below the Conowingo Dam.)
Massachusetts	None
Michigan	Lake St. Clair, Hamlin Lake, Bass Lake, Elk Skegemog, Six-Mile Lake, Craig Lake, Indian River, Lac Vieux Desert, Chicagon Lake, Tahquamenon River, Brevort Lake, Detroit River, St. Clair River.
Minnesota	Leech Lake, Winnibigoshish, Cass, Andrusia, Little Boy, Wabedo, Lake of the Woods, West Battle, Wolf, St. Croix River, Mississippi River, Woman, Rush (Chisago Cty.), Big Mantrap, Spider (Itasca Cty.), Baby.
Mississippi	None
Missouri	Pomme de Terre, Stockton (stocked 1975).
Montana	None
Nebraska	None
Nevada	None
New Hampshire	None
New Jersey	Delaware River
New Mexico	None
New York	St. Lawrence River, Chautauqua Lake, Allegany River, Conewango Creek, Olean Creek, Bear Lake, Cassadaga Creek, Middle Cassadaga Lake, Lower Cassadaga Lake.
North Carolina	French Broad River (lower), Little Tennessee River, Hiwassee River, Fontana Lake, Hiwassee Lake, Santeelah Lake.
North Dakota	Spiritwood, Lake Williams.

Ohio
Leesville Lake, Clear Fork, Pymatuning, Piedmont, Hargus, Rocky, Cowan, Lake White, Buckeye, Seneca, Clendening, Dillon, Knox, Delaware, Berlin, Highlandtown, Action, Salt Fork, West Branch, Jackson Lake, Sunfish Creek, Scioto Brush Creek, Rocky Fork Creek, Paint Creek.

Oklahoma
None

Oregon
None

Pennsylvania
Conneaut, Canadohta, Pymatuning, French Creek, LeBoeuf, Presque Isle Bay (Lake Erie), Allegheny River, Eaton Reservoir, Sugar, Edinboro, Schuylkill River, Opossum Creek Lake, Susquehanna River (main stem and north branch), Conestoga Cree, Hills Creek Lake, Juniata River, Delaware River, Lake Jean, Keystone Reservoir, Perkiomen Creek, Beltzville Lake.

Rhode Island
None

South Carolina
None

South Dakota
None

Tennessee
Dale Hollow Reservoir, Woods Reservoir, Norris Reservoir, Fort Patrick Henry Reservoir.

Texas
None

Utah
None

Vermont
Northern Lake Champlain, Missisquoi River (lower).

Virginia
Smith Mountain Lake, Burke Lake, Shenandoah River, James River.

Washington
None

West Virginia
Middle Island Creek, Little Kanawha River, Hughes River (main and south fork), Elk River, Bluestone Reservoir, Pocatalico River, West Fork Little Kanawha, McElroy Creek, Tygart River, Shenandoah River, Sutton Reservoir.

Wisconsin   Chippewa Flowage, East Twin, English,
                             Amnicon, Flambeau Flowage, Tur-
                             tle Flowage, Gile Flowage, Clear
                             Lake, Flambeau River (north and
                             south forks), Lac Court Oreilles, Lost-
                             land, Teal Lake, Big Arbor Vitae,
                             Lac Vieux Desert, and some 300 other
                             lakes and rivers which are considered
                             Class A or high quality muskellunge
                             waters.
Wyoming   None
Canada   Beautiful Lake, (Manitoba), St. Lawrence
                             River, Lake St. Clair, Kawartha
                             Lakes, (Ontario), Georgian Bay,
                             French River, Lake Nipissing, Lake
                             of the Woods, Nosbonsing, Eagle
                             Lake, Crow Lake.